For Cameron Boyle

A good friend is the most
precious of all possessions

Front cover: The Abbott and Shields streets intersection in Cairns, circa 1930. The Imperial Hotel, built in 1889, was destroyed by fire in 1945 and a temporary bar operated there until a new hotel opened in 1956. The Imperial closed its doors for trading on May 21, 1980 and was replaced by a row of shops. The Cenotaph in the middle of the intersection was erected in 1925 and was removed in February 1972 to the Esplanade outside the RSL.

Picture: Cairns Historical Society

Back cover: The Abbott and Shields streets intersection in Cairns in October 2007.

GROWING UP WITH CAIRNS

A MEMOIR BY ALAN HUDSON

Published by the proprietor
The Cairns Post Pty Ltd

ABN 79 009 655 752

24-26 Abbott Street
PO Box 126 Cairns
Queensland 4879
Australia

First published by
The Cairns Post Pty Ltd, 2007

ISSN 1322-8587

Publisher: Nick Trompf

Author: Alan Hudson

Editor: Catherine Lindsay

Art Director: Steve Whitfield

Picture contributors: *The Cairns Post*
photographers, Cairns Historical Society

Printed by GEON

The Cairns Post thanks the Cairns Historical
Society and its volunteers for the use of
photographs and help in research. We
particularly acknowledge the considerable
effort of Terry Fisk in verifying dates and details
in the Moments in Time entries.

The Cairns Post

ABOUT THE AUTHOR

Author Alan Hudson was born and educated in Cairns. He was editor of *The Cairns Post* from 1974-91. He has written four books on local history: two on South Johnstone and Tully sugar mills; *A Very Public Life*, the authorised biography of Mick Borzi; and *Tracks of Triumph*, on construction of the Kuranda Scenic Rail (1886-91).

Since 2003, Alan has written *The North I Knew*, a regular feature in *The Cairns Post*, on his memories of Cairns in his early years, on which this publication is heavily based. In July 2007, he became only the third person to be awarded the Cairns Historical Society's S.E. Stephens History Award for researching local history and presenting it to the public in a way that is readily understood.

FOREWORD

Editors of regional newspapers should be men and women who are passionate about where they live, and just as passionate about maintaining the credibility and objectivity of their newspaper's editorial content.

The Cairns Post enjoyed what I consider its halcyon years when Alan Hudson – a true newspaper man with printer's ink running through his veins – sat in the editor's chair, and set a standard for journalism that stood as a template for any country newspaper.

Alan went on to write several books after retiring from the newsroom in July 1991, but his editorial influence is still felt even to this day.

For the past five years, his skills as an accurate historian have been demonstrated through a series of very popular articles appearing in the *Post* under the title *The North I Knew*. Through this forum, Alan has introduced a whole new generation to the Cairns of the past. His stories have helped rekindle a spark of nostalgia in so many who have lived in the region for most of their lives, and still fondly remember the good old days when life truly was less complicated.

Cairns is steeped in history, carved out of mangroves and mudflats by pioneers who did it tough. Alan Hudson has captured scenes from the past through his vivid recollections and remarkable powers of observation and skills as a writer. For those more recently settled in the area, Alan's articles have given a good background into how our city has grown to become the thriving, international city it is today.

I cannot think of a better author for a title *Growing up with Cairns* than a local lad made good, who has helped make modern history so popular and enjoyable, and has opened so many windows to our past, allowing us all to gain a better understanding of where we have come from, and where we are heading.

Kevin Byrne
Cairns Mayor
November 2007

INTRODUCTION

Growing up with Cairns is a memoir of the city during the lifetime of the author Alan Hudson, born and bred local, a historian and former editor of *The Cairns Post* (1974-91).

Trinity Bay was recommended in 1873 by explorer George Dalrymple as an excellent harbour. It was settled in October 1876 after miners on the Hodgkinson goldfield, 145km west of Cairns, sought a more direct route to the coast to receive their goods that previously were transported by packhorse from Cooktown. Bill Smith blazed a trail to Trinity Bay in September 1876. An official party first came here on the SS Leichhardt. The first settlers, consisting of government officials and about 40 passengers, arrived from Townsville on the SS Porpoise on October 6, 1876. A larger party came from Cooktown two days later and some 300 people lived in two camps in the new settlement. The settlement was first known as Thornton after William Thornton, collector of customs in Brisbane, but it took its official name from the governor, William Wellington Cairns.

Cairns was to be the main port for mineral and timber reserves of the Atherton Tablelands. Initially goods were carried over the range along precarious pack horse routes, until the construction of Cairns-Kuranda railway in 1886-91. Cairns was built on a mangrove swamp. During construction of the Kuranda railway, soil from excavations was used to fill in the boggy sections of the town. Some 3 million cubic metres of earthworks were removed during construction of tunnels and cuttings. Much of this soil was brought into Cairns in 1888-89 on a temporary tram line that ran east along Shields St, and south down Abbott St to the wharves.

The new railway was built by Melbourne contractor John Robb with a workforce up to 1200. It gave Cairns the impetus to survive and opened the Tablelands and Outback for beef, dairying and other agricultural and horticultural pursuits as the mining boom began easing off into the 1900s. But by the end of 1877, it had fallen into depression in the face of competition from the booming township of Port Douglas, which attracted government offices and relocated business from Cairns. For elections in 1881, fewer than 90 names were on the Cairns rolls. Property values had slumped. Export of timber kept the township alive.

However, construction of the rail line, which eventually reached Herberton in 1911, provided Cairns with an economic lifeline. Built at a cost of at least $200 million in today's values, it was approved by the Queensland government to appease Herberton residents and their need for assured, all-weather transport to survive. It started a minor construction boom in Cairns and new buildings included the hospital (1884), St Monica's church (1886), the McLeod St railway station (1887) and Abbott St Customs House (1887-89).

Many new dwellings and boarding houses filled a need for rental accommodation. The subdivision of Parramatta Park, one of the city's first, was developed in 1886. It was named Parramatta Estate. It became known simply as Parramatta, but later was officially changed to Parramatta Park to avoid confusion with the Sydney suburb. A second building boom took place between 1907 and 1914 when a more diversified economy provided capital for private investment.

The Cairns stock exchange set up in 1906, mainly to deal in mining shares. Interest in tourism was increasing and substantial improvements were being made to port facilities with the Cairns Harbour Board (known as the Cairns Port Authority from 1984) coming into force on January 1, 1906. Work began in 1915 on new concrete wharves. Some 24 significant buildings were constructed during this surge in prosperity. They included the ambulance (corner Spence and Sheridan streets); Cairns Harbour Board offices at 1 Lake St; School of Arts (now Cairns Museum, Shields St); post office (corner Abbott and Spence); court house (Abbott St); The Cairns Post (Abbott St), Adelaide Steamship Co. (corner Spence and Lake streets); shipping company Howard Smith (Abbott St) and the three-storey Boland Centre (Spence and Lake). Some still stand today.

An early government decision to establish the Kamerunga State Nursery in 1889 was to provide benefits in agriculture and horticulture that surpassed the expectations of even *The Cairns Post* editor, who speculated that it "... cannot be other than beneficial to the selector or owner of land who requires to know what to grow and when to grow it". Early experimental crops included tea, vanilla, rubber, oil palms, fibre plants and Burmese teak, while badila, the outstanding cane variety used on North Queensland sugar farms for half a century, was trialled there in the 1890s.

It also helped to establish a viable coffee industry in the Kuranda area where some 60 growers worked 168ha of the crop before the industry faltered due to high labour costs and a severe winter frost in 1901. The nursery operated for 104 years, in later years trialling most of the tropical fruits now grown in the district, before closing in February 1993. Maize, rice, cotton, coffee, pineapples and bananas were among the early crops grown in the Cairns area pre-1900s.

But sugar, which is still the district's major industry with tourism, began to take over around the turn of the century. The first attempt to grow sugar commercially was made in 1879 by the Hop Wah (or Hap Wah) syndicate on a 240ha block in today's suburb of Earlville. It closed in 1886 due to a combination of low world sugar prices, inferior cane varieties and labour problems. Increasing amounts of bagged sugar manufactured at the Hambledon Mill at Edmonton, taken over by CSR in 1897, and others at Mossman, Mulgrave and Babinda, were shipped through Cairns and helped to provide revenue to develop port facilities.

The Cairns economy went through troughs and peaks in the early 1900s, but the population grew steadily until it reached 8000 in 1923, qualifying it to be declared a city. Cairns had been connected to the outside world only by sea until completion of the coastal railway to Brisbane with the official opening of a rail bridge at Daradgee, north of Innisfail, on December 10, 1924.

In 1930, Alan Douglas Hudson, the fourth of six children of Wilfred and Annie May Hudson, was born. From there we begin the story of *Growing up with Cairns*.

This is the only known photograph of Alan Hudson as a child. Alan (left) is with family members on an outing to one of Cairns's northern beaches, circa 1936.

Cairns in the 1930s, showing the Abbott and Spence streets intersection with the Koch memorial fountain in the centre, Bank of NSW in the right foreground and opposite the two-storey Commonwealth Bank on the corner section of Anzac Park.

CHAPTER ONE - 1930s

Cairns in 1930 was no more than a tropical outpost with about 9500 permanent residents. City streets were unpaved, bumpy and dusty mid-year, and with potholes filled with water in the wet. Tradesmen still used horse and cart to deliver goods, and bicycles were the main means of transport. The average worker was earning about £250 ($15,000 in today's money) a year, cigarettes were sixpence a packet of 10, houses in Draper and Martyn streets were advertised for under £500 ($30,000), and weekly rents for flats and houses ranged from 18 to 25 shillings ($55-75).

Newspapers were filled with depressing economic news in the wake of the Wall St crash of 1929. *The Cairns Post* reported that timber industry leaders sought a tariff on cheap imports from the Philippines which threatened the livelihoods of hundreds of workers in the Cairns district.

Cairns (later Mulgrave) Shire Council controlled the outer parts of the city when the Cairns City Council boundary was at a line with Fearnley St, just west of Cairns Showground. It was moved in 1940 to Chinaman Creek, just short of McCoombe St, then in 1956 to Clarke Creek, near today's

Stockland Earlville. The Hudsons were among many working class families that lived in the heavily populated residential Bunda and Draper streets area close to the city's biggest employers of blue collar labour: sawmills, brewery, wharves, railways and wholesale merchants. The main residential part of Cairns extended only as far north as Lily St and west to Aumuller St.

I was born on December 24, 1930 in a midwife's home in Lumley St, only a few hundred metres from the Cairns CBD. According to *The Cairns Post*, Christmas Day, the day after my birth, was celebrated much as it is today, with good attendances at churches, Christmas dinner served in homes and hotels, and at picnics at the beach. The paper reported: "Christmas was celebrated in almost perfect atmosphere. Occasional passing showers on Wednesday (Christmas Eve) only accentuated the geniality of the salubrious climate and cleared and cooled the air. The days were bright and fresh and the nights were delightful."

Homes of many working class families did not have access to the city's first electric power provided by a small steam

Many tradesmen in the 1930s were still using horse and cart to deliver their goods, including Sydney Edward Smith, who owned the West Cairns Dairy on his property opposite today's Raintrees Shopping Centre.

generating plant in McLeod St, which was connected on January 14, 1925. Families like the Hudsons used kerosene lamps for lighting, and cooked their meals on wood-fired stoves. My mother, like many women, boiled the family's clothes in disused four-gallon (16-litre) fuel tins over open wood fires before washing them by hand over concrete tubs attached to the back of the house. In days before the Hills Hoist, she hung our clothes on lines propped up by a branch we salvaged from nearby bushland.

We always had cold showers. Our one treat during winter was a warm bath on Sunday afternoons in a large galvanised washing tub in the kitchen. At least four Hudson siblings lined up in our house and always squabbled about who would have first use of the water, which was diluted after each use by a saucepan of boiling water. Too bad if you were last and had to dry off with the only threadbare towel available.

In our family, it was an unwritten law that the eldest non-working male child was responsible for keeping up the household wood supply. As the youngest of three sons, my turn came in 1942 when I was aged 11. Sources of wood were close at hand with two sawmills only a block or two away and the railway workshops and marshalling yards just across the road. One important task was to prepare the kindling (or "morning wood" as we knew it) so that my mother could start the stove burning at 6am every day. But too often I squirmed with guilt in my warm winter's bed when I heard my mother chopping away in the morning darkness after I had failed to do my job. All was forgiven an hour later as we huddled in the kitchen around the warmth of the wood stove to eat our breakfast. Many homes elected to use wood stoves even after electricity was connected.

Households managed well enough without refrigeration. I remember the red letter day when a neighbour gave us an old wooden ice chest. It had two compartments, one at top about 16 by 10 inches and eight inches deep (40cm by 25cm by 20cm) for the block of ice and the other larger part below to store perishables. I had to go to either of the two iceworks in Sheridan St, the Albion where the police headquarters is

today or Bennett's opposite Rusty's Markets, and carry it home quickly in a hessian sugar bag before it melted. It cost a shilling in the late 1930s and we could afford a block only on weekends and only during summer. We looked forward to our Sunday treat by setting a jelly and having it with a tin of sliced peaches and a dob of Nestle's thickened cream.

But most of the poorer homes did not store perishables. If my mother cooked a meat dish, she bought enough beef for a single meal that day from the local butcher and cooked it immediately. We bought items like fresh milk and butter in small quantities so that they would not have to be kept. We had fresh milk only with breakfast cereals then tinned condensed milk for cups of tea at other times. Some homes had a meat safe to store perishables. It was a small metal container with gauze or perforations in its walls to allow ventilation. It was hung from the ceiling or a crossbeam in the coolest part of the house, usually in some breezeway.

Most of today's inner suburbs of Bungalow, Portsmith, Westcourt and beyond were bush. As a child, I swam in a sandpit pool near today's intersection of Ogden and Hartley streets in Bungalow. It was given its name around 1910 after Archdeacon Joseph Campbell's home of the same name located there.

Dairy farms in what later became Cairns's inner suburbs provided milk for local residents. Albert and Ernie Dean had a dairy at Edge Hill; there was one in Lyons St on the southern side of Mulgrave Rd owned by Jack Veivers, who sold it to Dan Higgins in 1939-40; the Hoad family had another off Mulgrave Rd, near Earlville; and McMahons grazed their dairy herd on undeveloped land between Buchan and Aumuller streets, near Winkworth St. A farmer named Jones kept pigs and poultry on a large property on the north-western corner of Mulgrave Rd and Buchan St. Jones St, running parallel to Buchan St, is named after him.

Although the streetscape of the Cairns of the 1930s has been altered almost beyond recognition, the biggest change since my childhood has been in the lifestyle. No household that I knew had a telephone. If people wanted to

The Downey residence in Sheridan St, between Lily and Arthur streets, was typical of the average low-set houses in Cairns in the 1930s with their wide front verandahs to catch the breeze. Mrs Downey's son-in-law was Cecil Williams, who served as Mulgrave shire clerk for some years in the late 1930s and 1940s before becoming town clerk of the Cairns City Council.

Picture: Cairns Historical Society

communicate, they wrote a letter, even to someone living in the same town. If the matter was urgent they might send a telegram. But telegrams were received with great foreboding. There were few things more unsettling than to receive one, unless its arrival coincided with a birthday, wedding or special occasion. A telegram invariably meant bad news. Someone must have died or was critically ill. I can recall my mother staring for minutes at an unopened telegram, contemplating all kinds of ill-fortune that probably had befallen friends or family before she finally opened the envelope to learn that my elder brother Fred was arriving home unexpectedly on leave from war service. There were no public telephones on street corners. Calls in some desperate circumstances like a death in the family were made at the post office in Abbott St where it was booked and paid for in advance and often took up to 30 minutes to be connected.

Few households had a motor vehicle, and those who did filled their tanks with benzene, not petrol. Even a bicycle for some poorer families was a luxury. Most working class families of Cairns walked. Everywhere. If we wanted to get from one place to another, there was only one way to achieve it and that was by walking. We walked to school, we walked to work, we walked to sport or to leisure and entertainment. I attended school in Cairns for 11 years and, like hundreds of other kids of my time, I walked to and from school every single day, whether in the blazing sun or during a monsoonal downpour of rain. We thought nothing of it. It was a luxury to use a bus, let alone think of hiring a taxi.

As in other parts of the developed world, Cairns in the 1930s was going through the worst economic downturn in its short history. My father Wilfred was a carpenter. Even though I was then a small child, I vividly remember his anguish at knowing he could not find work to

Itinerant homeless men or "swaggies" as they were known, camped at buildings at Cairns Showground during the Great Depression years of the 1930s. It was the scene of an altercation known as The Battle of Parramatta Park when local citizens tried to evict them so that preparations for the 1932 Cairns Show could go ahead.

Picture: Cairns Historical Society

earn enough to feed his family of five school-age children.

Queensland's registered unemployed had shot up from about 10,000 in 1929, the year of the great Wall St crash, to more than 32,000 by June 1932. Regular dole payments, child endowment, single parent allowances and other forms of government welfare, were not available then.

Because of the hard times, the federal government in 1930 introduced a system of "relief" work. At a time when the average weekly wage was less than £5 ($300 in today's values), single men were paid the equivalent of £2/10/- (about $150) a week and married men £3 (about $180). To finance the scheme, the government ordered that every pay packet, share dividend or interest payment upwards from £1 (about $60 today) was levied at the rate of about 2.5 per cent.

But even the relief work was not enough to sustain the mounting numbers of unemployed in Australia. Thousands of workers, including married men and university graduates, took to the roads and went from town to town, tapping into one system after another in a hand-to-mouth system of survival, "swags" on their backs, hoping for a lift from motor vehicles going their way. Many "jumped the rattler", illegally riding on goods trains from one town to the next, a practice often overlooked by sympathetic railway supervisors and police officers. By the mid-1930s, hundreds of itinerants, or "swaggies" as we knew them, had made their way to

Far North Queensland looking for work, surviving on handouts most of the time.

For most, Cairns would have been the end of the line in their attempt to find work and they settled into makeshift shelters to contemplate their future. I remember how some lived in a shanty-type collection of rough shelters in Bungalow. One cluster of huts was in the bush just east of Buchan St, between Scott St and Mulgrave Rd, and another on the southern side of Spence St near today's Ogden St. These were on a bank of a large waterhole we knew as "The Sandpit" where we kids swam and launched canoes we made from old roofing iron. Huts were made of scrap timber and iron. Large hessian potato sacks were used to good effect as door screens, mats and bedding. A separate cooking area out front was covered by a piece of roofing iron as protection from rain.

In Cairns and other northern centres, churches helped to feed these nomadic men and the local council gave out as much work as its budget would allow. *The Cairns Post* published daily rosters for church guild members and other volunteers to operate soup kitchens and outlets where blankets and warm clothing were distributed.

Many homeless men found shelter at night in old huts, horse stalls and vacant buildings in the Cairns Showground that we knew as Parramatta Park.

It was the scene of a violent confrontation on July 16, 1932, when 34 police and 500 citizens forcibly evicted about 100 men so that preparations for the annual Cairns Show could proceed. The Battle of Parramatta Park, as it became known, resulted in some 80 people being injured with 10 of them serious enough to have been hospitalised.

Commercial aviation in the early 1930s was in its infancy. Tom McDonald, an Abbott St jeweller who settled here in 1923, set up the city's first airline soon after buying a Gypsy Moth in 1929, disillusioned by the lack of reliable transport by steamers from southern capitals. He used a saltpan at the southern end of today's Cairns International Airport, acquiring ashes from the local gasworks to pave a 100m strip. The Cairns City Council took control of the aerodrome in late 1930 and the next year up to 30 men worked there on improvements under a type of work for the dole scheme. McDonald was not only a legend in his lifetime, but a hero to children of my generation. I was one of dozens of kids in Cairns who would often play with arms outstretched, declaring "I'm Tommy Mac".

McDonald's airline traded initially as T.H. McDonald, but in October 1934 its name was changed to North Queensland

Airways when he floated the company. It provided passenger and freight services throughout North Queensland north to Thursday Island, regular services to Brisbane, and west to Mt Isa, calling at many centres in between. The trip from Cairns to Mt Isa began at 8.45am and arrived at the western township at 5.30pm. McDonald sold NQA to Airlines of Australia in 1938. However, he continued his association with aviation. He helped to form the Cairns Aero Club in March 1946 and his dedication to providing services to outback Far North Queensland and in times of great need is legendary. His daredevil feats knew no bounds if he was called on to help rescue anyone sick or injured and he flew in all kinds of weather all over North Queensland.

McDonald encouraged centres throughout North Queensland to become involved in commercial aviation and provide landing facilities. On one occasion, he flew his plane from Cairns to Ayr in July 1935 simply as a favour to a friend to test an aircraft owned locally by Bob Brown.

A Townsville newspaper once recorded a typical day's flying in a hectic schedule for McDonald in March 1936. He left Cairns in the morning on the tri-weekly service to Cooktown. After delivering his passengers and mail, he set out with a seriously ill patient, accompanied by a nurse, for

Shields St from the Abbott St intersection with the Imperial Hotel on the left corner and the Blue Bird cafe on the right, circa 1930s.

Tom McDonald, an Abbott St jeweller until his death in 1978, was the pioneer of Cairns aviation when he established his own airline in the early 1930s.

Atherton. On completion of this task, he flew back to Cairns to pick up a patient to be taken to Innisfail, returned to Cairns and loaded mail and passengers for Townsville, leaving that city the following day at 6am for Cairns and Cooktown.

On another flight to Brisbane in February 1936, McDonald amazed officials at Archerfield airport when he arrived soon after dawn, largely unscathed, after flying through a series of severe storms on the way down from Cairns. His aircraft had only a few patches of paintwork left and the propeller was so badly splintered it had to be replaced. He quickly dismissed anything heroic about his feat by declaring: "I am more or less used to bad flying weather in the north, but I never encountered anything like this before. Rain came down in torrents and visibility at times between Cairns and Townsville was impossible. It was just like flying through a wall of water. Visibility was rarely more than 200 yards and you had to know all the landmarks."

McDonald's service to the outback was linked to the Cairns Aerial Ambulance, which made its first trip on January 9, 1937 when McDonald brought a sick child from Cooktown to Cairns. One of his most amazing feats was the time in 1933 when a cyclone hit the pearling and beche-de-mer fleets in the Cooktown/Cape Tribulation area and a number of luggers were wrecked. Authorities asked McDonald to fly up and look for survivors. He was unable to use his flooded strip at North Cairns so his plane was taken with wings folded into town and he took off from the beach at the northern end of the Esplanade, near the Cairns Base Hospital.

The Aerial Ambulance closed on June 20, 1979, a year after McDonald's death at the age of 86, when it was handed over to the Royal Flying Doctor Service. In 42 years, it made 6341 trips, flying almost five million kilometres on its mercy missions. Tom McDonald's great contribution to aviation was recognised in the city's centenary year in September 1976, with the staging of the Tom McDonald $10,000 Centenary Air Race.

I passed a milestone in my life in January 1936 when I attended school for the first time, enrolling in the Year One class at Parramatta State School on the corner of Mulgrave Rd and Severin St. The head teacher then, and for some years later, was Don Campbell, a legendary figure in education in this region. His other contribution to the welfare of youth was as president of the Cairns Combined Schools Band. Parramatta, which opened in 1927, was the city's biggest school with an enrolment of close to 1000 at one stage of my time there up to the end of 1944. Some of my schoolmates became lifelong friends and leading figures in the community. Les Maunder in later years was principal of the family business of Maunder Electrics, and Allen Jones, whose older brother Ray was a railway porter who became a city alderman (1962-66) before representing the city as the State Member for Cairns from 1965-83.

Cairns's first school had opened at No. 51 The Esplanade in 1877 with an enrolment of 26 girls and 24 boys. The school transferred to Lake St on the site of today's Oasis Inn in 1885 as the State School of Cairns, but was later known as Cairns Central School, with a section each for girls and boys.

Among other Cairns schools opened over time were Cairns North which began its life on February 12, 1917, as Edge Hill State School. Its name was changed to Cairns North State School when a small school was built in Pease St in the late 1930s and took over the name of Edge Hill State School.

The first movie I saw was when my aunt, Kate Kelly, took me around 1936 to the old Gaiety Theatre. They were known then as "talkies", because sound films were still something of a novelty after the silent movie days. It was little more than a huge tin shed with bare concrete floor and reclining canvas seating. The Gaiety had opened on October 1, 1929 with the showing of a sound film, *The Red Dance* starring Delores Del Rio. In the early 1930s, it also had a mini golf course,

The State School of Cairns, known later as Cairns Central School, opened for the school year of 1885 on the site bounded by Aplin, Abbott, Florence and Lake streets. It was demolished in the mid-1990s to make way for the Oasis Inn.

A class at Parramatta State School during the 1930s when Alan Hudson attended.

The Cairns Pictures, built in 1914 on the corner of Abbott and Shields streets, was later named the Tropical Theatre. It was rebuilt in 1938-39 after a fire, and closed in 1972 before being demolished in 1976 to make way for the Tropical Arcade. Other Cairns movie theatres – before television caused a decline from the 1970s – were the Rex in Sheridan St, which opened in 1939 and closed around 1978, the Plaza at 108 Mulgrave Rd, which opened in 1940 and closed in December 1972. The Palace in Lake St, which opened around 1918-19 in an open air setting, was sold to Woolworths in 1966 and for a few years operated as the Cinema Capri. It is now a hostel.

a form of entertainment popular in Cairns at the time with another facility on the corner of Lake and Upward streets.

The Gaiety did not survive long after World War II. The first permanent silent movie theatre, the Lyric, opened in Spence St in 1913 with a program of short films. It soon changed its name to the Palace, then a new Palace Theatre opened in Lake St in 1914. The Cairns (later Tropical) Theatre, corner Abbott and Shields streets, was also built around this time. Both the Gaiety and the Palace in July 1931 had shown the first motion picture filmed entirely in Cairns when *The Adventures of Dot* premiered in the city. It was a story of a romantic triangle involving Dot, a new arrival in Cairns, and two men. Publicity for the movie promised "street scenes, delightful views of the Esplanade, the new city council chambers and many other landmarks".

The gloom of the depression years of the 1930s in Cairns was lightened when 4CA, the district's first local commercial station, began broadcasts in May 1936 from an old Queenslander at 8 Grove St, a site later occupied by the Masonic Bowls Club. 4CA had only one studio sound-proofed by Caneite (wall-sheeting) and hessian lining, and no form of airconditioning. From then on, families like the Hudsons huddled around their kitchen table at night to listen to their favourite shows, which included in later years *Dad and Dave*, Bob Dyer's quiz show *Pick-a-Box*, a variety program with Jack Davey, Hal Lashwood and comedian Roy (Mo) Rene, *Australia's Amateur Hour* compered by Harry Dearth and Dick Fair, and the one-hour drama presented on the Lux Radio Theatre on Sunday at 8pm.

In the late 1930s, 4CA began transmitting at 7.30am with a 15-minute news service from *The Cairns Post* at 7.45am, following by the *Mother's Session* at 8am. The station closed at 9am, and reopened at noon with *Midday Melodies*. It closed again at 2pm, reopened at 5.30pm, and closed for the day at 10pm. Later, 15-minute news bulletins were relayed by landline to 4CA from the south at 7.45am, 12.30pm and 7pm, and the popular serials that included *Martin's Corner*, *Big Sister* and *When a Girl Marries*.

Doreen Dean, Mavis Meade, Betty Errington and Betty Reece were popular comperes of the station's morning program in the early years. There were no phone-in facilities in those days, but loyal listeners joined the 4CA Women's Club in their droves and often wrote letters that were acknowledged on air. 4CA moved in the 1950s to larger offices in Shields St on the floor above Clauson's Jewellers, and more recently to its present location in Virginia House, 68 Abbott St.

Sachs (later Grafton) St, between Spence and Shields, held a fascination for children of my age in the 1930s. It was known then as Chinatown, occupied by shops, illegal gambling dives, opium dens and brothels. Chinese moved to Cairns when gold ran out near Cooktown in the 1870s. In the early 1930s, the 1376 Chinese living here made up about 17 per cent of the city's population. Some became merchants or small shopkeepers, setting up business in areas in Cairns, Atherton and Innisfail.

The Chinese fruit and vegie man was a familiar sight as he sold his wares door-to-door from baskets balanced either end of a pole slung across his shoulders, or from a small two-wheeled cart he pushed around the local streets. The fellow who called at our place always left us a Christmas gift, usually a small packet of crystallised ginger, a real treat for us. Some grew their own produce. I remember at least one market garden in Sachs Sts. More than 50 Chinese merchants traded in Cairns by the early 1900s. Apart from its shopkeepers, Sachs St once had a Chinese hospital and two temples, commonly known as joss houses.

Sachs St prospered until about 1915 when a decline began, reflected partly in some Chinese moving out and an increasing influx of Japanese and Europeans. The exodus continued through the 1930s and, during World War II, only a few Chinese traders remained in an area better known for its brothels. The former Anglican Bishop of Cairns George Tung Yep lived there as a child when his father Yee Tung-yep was partner in the firm of Sam Sing, one of the longest

The staff of 4CA in 1946: (Back row from left) John Young, Bill Cunningham, Mavis Meade, Geoff Callaghan, Betty Reece, Tony Studdert and Lesley Ross. (Front from left) Betty Waugh, manager John Dower, John Gleeson and Joan Tills.

4CA, the district's first local commercial radio station, began broadcasts in May 1936 from this old Queenslander in Grove St.

Cairns Show was always a time for locals to dress in their Sunday best as shown by Mr and Mrs John Gibson and family, circa 1938.   Picture: Cairns Historical Society

Pony-sized Johnnie Graham, ridden by George Crook, was the idol of Cairns Show crowds during the 1930s.

running merchants in Cairns's Chinatown. Chinatown's conversion to a more traditional business area began in the 1940s. The Exchange Book Shop, still operating there, opened its doors at 78 Grafton St in 1942, and Bob and Ron Norman started their Perfection Dry Cleaners over the road at No. 75-79 in 1946.

But the street still had its brothels and its seedy reputation and PDC's business did not take off until police began moving the prostitutes out. Snowy Cox and Bob Allwood were among the illegal SP bookies who had their betting shops there, and later a milk bar, restaurant, De Luxe Taxis, McDonalds (later G.K. Bolton) Printers were among several businesses on the eastern side of the street. The Trocadero Dance Palais relocated from the Mazlin building in Lake St to the western side of Grafton St late in 1954. Cairns City Council, acting on a complaint from a resident of Sachs St about negative connotations of its name as being associated with prostitution, on June 16, 1936 agreed to rename Sachs St as Grafton St. Legend has it that one alderman wanted the new name to be Hoare St after a previous mayor, probably not realising his gaffe until he said it out loud.

As a child of the 1930s, I will always associate the name of Johnnie Graham with the Cairns Show. Johnnie Graham was a pony owned by the McHardie family of Edmonton who captured the hearts of people in this region in the 1930s with his high-jumping exploits, often outperforming bigger horses at district shows. His sudden death in September 1938 caused a pall of gloom to descend over the Far North and tributes in newspapers at the time would have done justice to the most loved and respected community figure.

Going to Cairns Show in my childhood was a family affair. Mum, dad and the kids dressed in their Sunday best, women always with hat, gloves and handbag, dad in his one and only suit, and a rare occasion when kids wore shoes. They all happily posed for a photographer positioned outside or just inside the main entrance. Expectations were modest and a few shillings I earned selling soft drink bottles and old newspapers to the corner store, or one year when I received a penny each for selling programs at greyhound races, were enough for a grand day's entertainment. We were usually satisfied with a toffee apple, a wad of fairy floss, a creamy waffle or two, and a few rides on Dodgem cars, tilter whirl or ferris wheel, as well as a walk through sideshow alley, enjoying the banter of spruikers and ogling the pretty girls. Watching the W.J. Houston high jump and the grand parade on the third and final day (always Thursday in those days) was mandatory, and a visit to Jimmy Sharman's tent was a must to delight in Jimmy's raucous challenges to the local toughs and ringers from outback cattle stations to try to survive three rounds with one of his boxers and earn a couple of quid.

An unusual event of the late 1930s was the creation in the wet season of late 1939 of a realignment of the mouth of the Barron River, according to a report from the district land officer in Cairns, dated November 16, 1939. The officer recommended that informal lease No. 1423 be written off the books of the department after the lessee called at its Cairns office to state that the leased land, with improvements, had been washed away by a flood. The old outlet 1.5km south of Ellie Point had silted over completely and became colonised by mangroves.

The decade of the 1930s ended on a desperate note when World War II began with the declaration of hostilities against Germany on September 3, 1939. While the war in Europe had a minor physical impact on the Cairns district, loved ones from many local families volunteered for the armed services, including my father, Wilfred Douglas Hudson, QX7791. He advanced his birth date by a year and enlisted on June 15, 1940, aged 40, and served in the Middle East until his discharge on medical grounds in January 1943.

Ironically, although the allotment to families from a meagre soldier's pay was only a few shillings a week, it provided many households, including ours, with the first steady income they had for some time after the uncertainty of employment during the Great Depression years of the 1930s.

MOMENTS IN TIME

1930 – August 11
New Council Chambers open in Abbott St, site of today's City Library.

1931 – July 1
Premiere of *The Adventures of Dot*, first motion picture shot entirely in Cairns.

1932 – July 16
Aviator Charles Kingsford Smith (right) lands his aircraft Southern Cross in Cairns.

1933 – December 17
Cook Highway between Cairns and Port Douglas officially opens.

1935 – June
Cane toad is introduced from Hawaii at Gordonvale to assist in natural control of greyback beetle infesting sugar cane crops.

1935 – November 20
Barron Falls Hydro Electricity Scheme switched on.

1936 – May 16
4CA, first commercial radio in Cairns, first broadcasts from studios at 8 Grove St.

1939 – November 16
Heavy silting forces relocation of mouth of Barron River from Ellie Point to Casuarina Point, just south of Machans Beach.

A.J. DRAPER - THE FATHER OF CAIRNS

An Abbott St business which closed in 1966 was the last visible link with Alexander Frederick John Draper, the man known as "The Father of Cairns". Draper died in 1928, almost three years before I was born, but the A.J. Draper legend was alive and well long after his death and no wonder: no Cairns citizen, in his time or since, has ever occupied a position of prominence in civic and community affairs as he did.

The business that Draper established continued to flourish into the 1960s as A.J. Drapers in Abbott St, opposite the court house, and at one time was the single biggest employer in the city with more than 100 people working there. Drapers were accountants, tax consultants, auctioneers and valuers, as well as complete home furnishers.

They made furnishings at the Abbott St premises or in factories elsewhere in the town. Mattresses were made at Abbott St before transferred to a building in Bunda St, around the present entrance to *The Cairns Post's* press room. Their furniture factory was also in Bunda St, on the corner of Hartley St. It was destroyed by fire in the early 1950s and thereafter was located near the Migrant Centre in Bungalow.

Former Cairns mayor Ron Davis worked at Drapers in Abbott St from the time he started as a junior in 1942 until its closure. Drapers closed after it was sold to AMP in 1966 and Woolworths was established on the site.

A.J. Draper also owned The Cairns Post Pty Ltd. After a failed venture with the *Cairns Chronicle*, his younger brother, Edward ("Hoppy"), an experienced journalist, started *The Cairns Morning Post* in 1895, and when he died in 1901, the paper was left to A.J. But it had always been A.J.'s energy and business skills that drove the paper. *The Post* was still owned by the Draper family when it was sold to Queensland Press Ltd, owners of *The Courier-Mail*, in November 1965.

Draper was mayor of Cairns for single-year terms in 1891-93, 1897, 1902, 1918-19, and finally in 1924-27 just after three-year terms were introduced. Draper was defeated for the mayoralty in the 1927 election won by W.A. (Billy) Collins, who went on to be the city's longest serving mayor for 22 years until 1949. There was no separate election in those days, with the candidate polling the most votes becoming mayor. One of Draper's proudest moments was the celebration of Cairns's jubilee during the first week of November 1926 during his time as mayor. Many citizens regarded the event as Draper's greatest triumph, but he said it was a time to honour the city's pioneers and he and Mrs

Draper lavishly entertained 20 people, among them those who had landed on the day in 1876 Cairns was proclaimed a settlement and others who arrived soon after.

Draper was born in Melbourne on April 5, 1863, the first of 17 children to Captain Henry Draper and his wife, Ellen. He joined the Bank of Australasia after leaving school in 1879, and after appointments to Beechworth and Bethanga, both in Victoria, he was posted to Jerilderie (NSW) where he met Mary Georgina Capron, his future wife. He was sent north to Townsville as accountant of the branch there, then to busy Charters Towers in 1884, where at only 20 years of age, he became acting manager.

Draper arrived in Cairns on June 26, 1884, to take charge of the Bank of Australasia's branch. The Drapers lived for 35 years at Lilybank, a 64ha property at Freshwater where six of their seven children (all girls) were born. The eldest child, Henry, died in July 1891 when a cartridge he was playing with exploded, causing fatal injuries. While Lilybank was renowned for its beauty as a country residence, Draper threw his energies into making it productive. For some years, he

sent 600-1000 cases of pineapples to southern markets. He also tried to grow thousands of young fruit trees, including peaches, apples and pears imported from Victoria, but without success. He was involved in horse-breeding and sold a number of animals bred at Lilybank to southern interests.

Draper was appointed managing director of the Mulgrave Mill in May 1897 and was chairman until his death in 1927. After he died, the mill erected memorial gates in his honour and they stand there today. Despite his busy life, A.J. found time to be a loving and devoted husband and father to wife Mary and their seven children. Right up to the eve of his departure for Brisbane where he would spend his last days, Draper was thinking of another way in which he could serve the community of Cairns. On March 8, 1928, he attended a meeting of the recently formed Cancer Campaign Committee. When volunteers were invited, Draper was the first to offer his services, "in any way you like", he said. He left Cairns the next morning for Brisbane to represent the region on extended sugar industry business. He died suddenly from a heart attack at 11.30pm on March 21, 1928, aged 64.

A.J. Draper's business in Abbott St, pictured mid-right, continued to flourish long after his death in 1929. Drapers were the single biggest employers in the city with more than 100 employees. They were accountants, tax consultants, auctioneers and valuers, and complete home furnishers, making most furnishings locally. They closed in 1966 and Woolworths now is located on the site.

Cairns in the late 1940s was easing back into its laidback lifestyle after the hectic years of the Pacific War (1942-45) when several locations in the city and many of its buildings were occupied by thousands of Australian and American service personnel.

CHAPTER TWO - 1940S

The Japanese invasion of Pearl Harbour on December 7, 1941 changed the laidback lifestyle of Cairns forever. With a real threat of invasion in the early months of 1942 following the fall of Singapore and the bombing of Darwin, civilians were urged to evacuate. Special passes were issued to residents north of Tully. Many families moved to Brisbane and beyond. Some sold their properties at bargain basement prices and never returned.

The family of a good friend, John D'Arcy, later financial director of Queensland Newspapers and CEO of the *Herald & Weekly Times* in Melbourne, sold their home in Sheridan St near the corner of Shields St. They went to Brisbane and stayed there. With my father away on active service, we Hudsons stayed put in our rented home in Bunda St, not out of bravado: we simply could not afford to move. But I was sent away for a few months in 1942 to stay with my uncle and aunt, Bob and Mary Hudson, on their dairy farm at Butchers Creek, where I attended school. New rationing regulations were imposed on civilians to cope with the huge wartime demands placed on both agricultural producers and manufacturers. Petrol rationing was introduced in 1940 and, in 1942, personal identity cards for adults and ration books for clothing and food were issued. The new rationing regulations included food items such as meat, tea, butter and sugar as well as clothing and footwear. We took our ration book to the shop and, for any of these items, the shopkeeper cut out the required number of coupons stipulated by law.

For most of 1942, Cairns schools were closed. Children did their lessons by correspondence. They went to my school, Parramatta, every Tuesday to collect assignments for the week ahead and turned in completed lessons from the previous week. A few of my classmates went by free railmotor to Woree where the school remained open. I went there for a few days, but quickly reverted to part-time

Cairns residents supported the war effort enthusiastically during World War II. Several groups of volunteers included the Women's Emergency Corps, pictured here being led by Monica Gabasa (nee Bimrose) down Lake St on Anzac Day 1941.

schooling at Parramatta, mainly to enjoy the extended leisure time, until I went to Butchers Creek.

Cairns was soon converted into a busy army town with service personnel from Australia and the United States using the city as a base. It would be flippant to suggest that World War II was anything but a time of upheaval, anxiety and sorrow for most Australian families. But for a lad a couple of weeks short of his 11th birthday when the Japanese bombed Pearl Harbour, I cannot recall feeling any sense of imminent danger in Cairns.

In fact, the war years were the most exciting of my young life with the old town abuzz with the frenzied activity of thousands of American and Australian servicemen and women, and more uniforms on show than I have ever seen.

But who could forget a war was on with those Catalina flying boats stationed in Cairns from 1942-44. They flew 3000 bombing missions out of Trinity Inlet. It was only many years later that I learned 320 of those brave airmen lost their lives in those sorties over enemy territory in and around New Guinea. Barracks of the HMAS Kuranda naval base were

built on reclaimed land about where today's bus terminal is at the eastern end of Spence St for Royal Australian Navy operations and the Catalina flying boat squadron.

At the peak of operations, HMAS Kuranda had a complement of 380, but by January 1945 it had been reduced to minor naval base status with only about 100 men serving there. Some officers were accommodated in the Hayles family's flats at the northern corner of Shields St and the Esplanade. The buildings were occupied after the war by various local community groups, including fishermen, lifesavers, rowers and other organisations as their clubhouses. The fishermen's hall was a popular venue that was available for hire for wedding receptions and other social events.

Our airport became an important refuelling and maintenance point for wartime aircraft. I remember going out there with hundreds of other locals to inspect a giant B-29 Superfortress that was on a tour of Australia to generate interest in a new issue of War Bonds.

Censorship was obviously effective, too. For instance, I had only a faint recollection of news of Darwin being bombed

Catalina and Martin Mariner flying boat aircraft were stationed in Trinity Inlet from 1942-44. They flew 3000 bombing missions and 320 brave airmen lost their lives in sorties over enemy territory in and around New Guinea.

Picture: Cairns Historical Society

Eleanor Roosevelt, wife of US president Franklin D. Roosevelt, visited Cairns in September 1943. She was one of several VIPs and show business personalities, including movie actor John Wayne, who visited Cairns during World War II to entertain troops stationed in the city.

Picture: Cairns Historical Society

in February 1942. I was horrified to learn years into my adulthood that 240 people were killed and hundreds injured in the raids. Most households had their own air raid shelter. We put a lot of effort into making a dugout in the backyard of our rented home in Bunda St from old corrugated roofing iron. It would not have been much use in a bombing raid as it was filled with water for weeks at a time. Many public shelters were built around the town. One, at the southeast corner of Munro Martin Park, remains today.

My mates and I quickly found that the American camps were a great source of comic books and magazines. Occasionally, we would score some "candy" (confectionery), particularly from one camp in Sheridan St where the police and law courts are now. We also spent time with Aussie troops attached to an Australian transport unit stationed at 187 Bunda St in a large residential building that today offers backpacker accommodation.

There was usually an open-air concert with topline acts every week at one of the several camps. I attended one at North Cairns sports reserve, and another in Mulgrave Rd near

the present Pacific Toyota premises.

Many of Australia's best musicians and entertainers performed in concerts at Cairns. I cannot remember any names, but I know we enjoyed them. A few American celebrities came to town to entertain their troops, including comedian Joe. E. Brown and actor John Wayne.

The end of World War II was announced in *The Cairns Post* on August 16, 1945 with a banner headline across the front page that read "Pacific war ends". It gained more prominence than the start of the war which Cairns people read on the fifth page at a time when the *Post*, like most papers throughout the world, had classified advertisements on their front page. *The Cairns Post* started running news on its front page from its January 2, 1945 edition when its main headline was "Hitler believes Germany won't lose war".

Most people remember what they were doing when important events in their lives happened. I recall exactly where I was when the Japanese surrender to end World War II took place. It was a Wednesday, and we were on school holidays. I was at 11 Lumley St, where my mate Ron

Cairns celebrated the end of World War II with a procession through city streets. Church bells rang, sirens sounded and spontaneous celebrations broke out when the war's end was announced on the wireless.

Beecheno lived, when word came through on the wireless that the war was over. It was late morning, and I think it might have been news of the Japanese offer of unconditional surrender, rather than the official announcement the next day. My reaction on hearing of the war's end was to take off like a startled hare to run the couple of hundred metres to our home at 169 Bunda St and share the news with my mother and two younger sisters. As in thousands of other Australian homes, it was not only a reason for celebration for us but a joyous and emotional time knowing a loved one would be coming home safely. In our case it was Fred, the oldest of six Hudson children, serving in Borneo with the RAAF.

The Cairns Post brought out a limited broadsheet edition that afternoon to announce the news, probably the first-ever special issue of the newspaper that has been produced. I remember the spontaneous celebrations in Cairns that day

with church bells ringing and sirens sounding, and perfect strangers embracing one another in a scene described by a report in *The Cairns Post*: "The morning's celebrations, entirely unorganised, were yet impressive by their very spontaneity. With one accord, the people rushed to the streets, linked arms with the nearest passerby and ran round and round the block shouting to their heart's content. For over two hours, the impromptu procession continued round and round the block (Abbott, Shields, Lake and Spence streets), gathering more trucks as it went until at one stage there were dozens of vehicles in the procession."

About 5000 people gathered in the Cairns City Council grounds in Abbott St (now the city library) that night to take part in community singing and dancing and, at 10.30pm, most of them danced around the main city block, led by two of our local brass bands.

It has been forgotten by many that a large civilian workforce was also part of the war effort in Cairns during World War II. Men aged 18 to 40, unfit for active duty and not employed in essential industries, were ordered by Manpower, which controlled Australia's wartime civil labour force, to report to either the Allied Works Council (AWC) or Civil Construction Corps (CCC). Projects tackled by this civil workforce included infrastructure to house troops, and building roads and airstrips.

When the Tablelands became a military headquarters with about 80,000 troops stationed there, road construction became necessary and the link from Cairns through Kuranda to Mareeba had a priority as an alternative to the more frequently used Gillies Highway.

Work on the Kuranda-Mareeba road started in the wet season. To lay a strip of bitumen and cover it with screening took 20 minutes, and this would hold up more than 100 vehicles at each end. Sidetracks through rough bushland were out of the question. More than 100 men were employed on these works which included widening the low-level bridge over the Barron River at Kuranda.

Projects of this civil workforce also included upgrading established aerodromes and building new airstrips at Cairns and Mareeba, one at Carpentaria Downs near Einasleigh, and others at Wrotham Park, Normanton, Inverleigh, Augustus Downs, Cooktown, Coen, Iron Range, Jacky Jacky at the tip of Cape York, and Horn Island.

Typical of the enterprise these people showed was at Mareeba where I was fascinated to read in a Main Roads Commission report of WWII activities that they were directed to have the Mareeba airstrip ready for the use of heavy bombers within eight days. The nearest MRC plant was at Herberton, but the feat was accomplished: a strip 2255m by 62m was ready for use within the time specified. Then a second strip of similar size was laid with a sealed taxiway between and buildings erected for administration and camps and facilities for the forces. Up to 700 men were employed on this work. Suitable screenings for bitumen work were

Allied Works Council staff spread fresh bitumen in upgrading work on the Cairns airport runway in 1940 during World War II. Herb Bird, who later settled in Mareeba, was the owner-driver of the 1937 Chevrolet Mapleleaf which carried gravel for the work from a quarry at Edge Hill.

These two naval oil fuel tanks were built into the hillside at Edge Hill for protection during World War II. The reinforced concrete tanks and three other fuel storage tanks elsewhere in the city were built in 1943 by the Allied Works Council (AWC) and Civil Construction Corps (CCC). The Edge Hill tanks were linked to the Cairns wharves with almost 5500m of 30cm piping.

unobtainable in the immediate area, so a method was used of washing and screening local quartz deposits to produce many thousands of cubic metres. These enterprising people solved the problem of laying the dust from the screenings by spraying them with a mixture of one part molasses and four of water. As many as four squadrons totalling 100 aircraft began to use the Mareeba field.

One of the major projects in Cairns was construction of the five fuel tanks in Collins Avenue, Edge Hill. A pipeline to the city's wharves ran from Edge Hill through Little and Draper streets. Three concrete tanks and two smaller steel tanks were built in Cairns in 1943 by the AWC and CCC to store motor and aviation spirit and naval oil fuel.

Two naval oil tanks at Edge Hill were linked to the Cairns wharves with 5500m of 30cm piping. Some 180 men worked on the project. The tanks were camouflaged by their position against the Whitfield range in a heavy canopy of trees and were thought to be relatively safe, compared with the city's other fuel storages located then, and for many years after, at the southern end of Grafton and Sheridan streets.

There were several AWC camps in Cairns. One was on the corner of McLeod and Spence streets, another larger one at North Cairns near Good Counsel School with 57 accommodation huts and other buildings later taken over by the army.

Other major AWC camps were at Stratford on a site of today's sewerage works where men were accommodated in 20-person huts on the Stratford Bowls Club site, and at Woree, Edmonton, and several locations on the Tablelands and throughout Cape York when projects were under way.

Two well-known Cairns men who helped to organise the huge civil workforce and the machinery and other equipment they used were C.B. (Bill) Headrick and Basil Creedy. Headrick – who at the time was working as a salesman/clerk in the family business, Headrick Pty Ltd in Spence St, managed by his father Dave – was appointed as the AWC's impressments officer here (impressment means

"forced into public service"). Creedy, a first grade rugby league player in his youth in Brisbane, was seconded from the State Government Insurance Office (now Suncorp) to take charge of the Manpower office in Cairns. He was later a city alderman and deputy mayor.

Headrick was authorised in May 1942 to carry out requisition of vehicles, tractors, concrete mixers and other equipment to be used by the civil workforce in the war effort. He had access to a list of all tractors, trucks and utes registered with the MRC since 1939 and, when a certain piece of equipment was needed, he would check the list and decide which one to take. He was well known to farmers and had to confiscate some of their essential equipment. He decided to "impress" one tractor in every three. All machinery was sent to Townsville where it was valued. Debate over payment was between Archie Graham, an AWC officer in Townsville, and the owner.

Creedy, as Manpower officer in Cairns, worked from an office at 6 Abbott St. Apart from the hundreds of men working for the AWC and CCC, Creedy had to oversee allocation of workers to other areas, including the waterside and the American services. Between 1942 and 1944, his office issued some 900 clearances to men and women to work for the Americans in the Cairns district, and about the same number for the wharves. Many preferred to work for the Americans because they paid higher wages.

My sister Betty, then in her late teens, worked for the American Red Cross in a building in Spence St near today's Pacific International. A job that civilian workers helped the American engineers on was building several Quonset huts, or igloos as we knew them, which were in use in Cairns and district for many years after the war. Another task the Americans undertook was building a concrete-paved road in Aumuller St between Spence St and the Smith's Creek for heavy traffic using it. They had a huge concrete-paving machine to mix the concrete and lay and level it, all in a single operation.

The original Cairns State High opened in 1924 as Cairns High School and Technical College. It was previously a secondary department at Cairns Boys State School in Lake St and was replaced by the present building in 1940.

Creedy also helped to provide a workforce for the cane cutting season, seconding experienced former sugar industry workers from the armed services for about five months. Single women under 40 also came under Manpower control, but they were paid at only one-third of the male wage.

Although the Curtin government tried to equalise the wages, it was opposed in the arbitration court by employers. Early in 1942, all wages and prices were frozen. House and shop rents were pegged. The freeze was not lifted until the 1950s. Creedy's work as Manpower officer ended in 1944.

The final years of World War II coincided with my move to Cairns State High late in January 1945 after I graduated by successfully passing the 1944 State Scholarship Examination after my nine years at Parramatta State School. I have nothing but pleasant memories of that time at Parramatta, but how drab and dull the classrooms were, how bland and uninteresting the lessons learned by rote, repeating words and mathematical tables written on blackboards (ironically green in colour).

We had airless, dimly-lit rooms and not even overhead fans, let alone modern comforts like airconditioning. In classes of 40 or more, five children shared a single desk seated on a wooden bench with no back-rest. Desks had an ink well for each place and vertical slot where slates were lodged when not in use. In early "prep" (preparatory) classes, children wrote on a slate, about 18cm wide by 24cm, edged with a thin wooden border. They wrote with a special slate pencil in a holder made of tin. Writing was erased with a damp sponge. The thought of a room with 40 children scratching away on their slates still puts my teeth on edge. We graduated to books from Grade One, writing day lessons in pencil and using ink for weekend homework exercises of essays and drawing maps.

Players in Cairns State High's 1945 rugby league team did not wear boots because of the austere wartime conditions. The 1945 Cairns High rugby league team: (from left standing) co-coach Bernard Mulcahy, Lionel Potts, Les Riggall, Jim Bourner, principal John McGrath, Bill Hodgon, Ray O'Rourke, Alan Medlock, co-coach Neville Corfield; (seated) Ernie Hondros, Alan Hudson, Jack Greene, Beres McKeown (c), Stan Sharpe, John Hird and John Gibb.

Most of us, even some girls, went to school for all of those nine years in bare feet. Shoes and uniforms were not required, nor could the Hudsons have afforded them. In the first few years of primary school, most lads of my age wore braces to hold up their knickers. Wearing a belt was considered a grownup thing to be aspired to when we were aged about 10. Shorts with elasticised waistbands and drawstring ties would not be designed for many years. We were not aware then of the dangers of skin cancer from too much exposure to the sun, but many lads wore "airway" hats, selling in 1938 for ninepence each. They were made from pandanus straw and had narrow cloth bands around the rim. But with the rough treatment boys gave them, they quickly became tattered with bits of straw sticking out everywhere. We had our own name for them: "donkey's breakfast".

We had no organised sport, mainly I suspect because of austere war conditions. The school had some sporting gear but we had no teacher supervision or coaching for games. We played cricket to our own rules before school and during lunch breaks. In winter, we kicked a footy around or played informal matches. If we wanted to use the school's two tennis courts, we could borrow racquets and balls. Teachers without exception were dedicated and respected. A few we feared, especially those who were fond of pelting a piece of chalk or a blackboard duster to attract a child's attention. Our male teachers at Parramatta included the handsome young dasher named Mr Hunter who joined the RAAF and went off to war; the kindly but sombre "Johnno" Johnston, an image not helped by dark, bushy eyebrows; and the delightful Mr Donald Peiniger, a grandfather figure right down to a habit of peering at us over spectacles balanced on the tip of his nose.

Then there was the memorable and formidable Jock Menzies, who taught us in Grade 7 in our final year at Parramatta. Prematurely grey in his early 40s, Mr Menzies was solidly built in the mould of the rugby league forward that he had been when he represented Cairns in his younger life. His personal crusade was for every member of our class to pass the Queensland Scholarship Examination, necessary for entrance to high school and, excellent teacher that he was, he lifted the benchmark for all of us, and not only our stellar performers, Eva Peirce and Ron Beecheno, who were among the best in Queensland.

There were always special teachers we loved and whose attention we craved. My favourites were Mollie Malone and Ina Parker, middle-aged spinster types so typical of schooling the world over. Some years later, I met Miss Malone in the street when holidaying in Toowoomba where she then lived. She recognised me instantly, greeted me warmly and rattled off the names of several classmates she wanted to hear about.

Drab classrooms, dull lessons? Yet I see myself on my final day in December 1944, turning my head at the Severin St gate for a final look back at my beloved Parramatta. A little tearful, I knew a special period of my life was over.

And so it was on to Cairns State High which then, well before TAFE colleges were introduced, also had a technical college attached where apprentices did their trade training. Cairns High had its start in 1917 when a secondary department was added to the Cairns Boys State School, or Cairns Central, where the Oasis Resort was built in Lake St in the mid-1990s. Students had to sit an entrance exam in December 1916 and the first enrolment included children from Innisfail, Tolga and Gordonvale. The first Cairns High School and Technical College on the present site in Sheridan St opened for the 1924 school year. The old wooden structure used then was replaced by the first of the present buildings in 1940.

High school meant an upgrade in standards for us. We were required to, and we did, wear shoes and socks for the first time after our nine-year barefoot stint at Parramatta. We also wore uniforms: navy shorts and white shirt and a tie with broad slanted navy and white stripes for boys and a similar ensemble for girls. The dress code alone was an uplifting experience and instilled in us a pride in ourselves and our school. Classrooms now were light and airy after the dingy rooms at Parramatta, and we had individual desks and seats with backing made of polished wood. I enrolled in the commercial stream, predominantly female, while many of my mates studied academic subjects. The basic difference was that my stream took bookkeeping, typing and shorthand with chemistry and physics in theirs, and standard subjects like geography, history, a language (French or Latin), maths, algebra and geometry for both.

But we still had few extra-curricular activities because of wartime restrictions, with very little organised sport, field trips or musical and theatrical opportunities. We had an annual swimming carnival and one year an athletics carnival, and in 1946 school army cadets were introduced. The only footy matches we played in my two years there were against Innisfail State High in 1945. We played in bare feet. The only other thing I remember about the Innisfail match was travelling down on the back of a truck driven by a teacher.

The return encounter was played one Saturday morning soon after at Parramatta Park. I do recall one incident from that match. I was picked as hooker, probably because I was the youngest member of the side. A scrum packed near halfway just before fulltime and we were trailing by a point or two. Innisfail won the ball and when I lifted my head from the scrum, I saw our five-eighth Bill Hodgon streaking away with the ball to score between the posts to win the game for us. Hodgon came up to me later and told me he was sure I would not win the scrum so he planned to intercept the pass from the Innisfail halfback to his five-eighth. It was clever thinking but not very flattering of my prospects as a rugby league hooker.

We were allowed in the 1945-46 summer to enter a cricket team in the local junior competition in which I took an enthusiastic part. But although the school provided the gear, we had no coaching or other teacher involvement: players had to organise everything. How different it was only a decade or so later when Cairns High had eight cricket XIs, and four rugby league and 12 hockey teams playing in local fixtures, and all kinds of other sporting, musical, theatrical and cultural activities on offer.

Alan Hudson's education at Cairns State High was disrupted in 1946 when he spent two weeks in Cairns Base Hospital with a severe bout of dengue fever, followed by several weeks of convalescence at home.

Still, we were always glad of the teachers we had then, including principal John McGrath, so immaculately turned out in a suit; Jock Menzies, our former scholarship teacher at Parramatta; Jack O'Shea; Neville Corfield; Bernard Mulcahy; Ms Fletcher; Dorothy Bonning; Vera Basket; Louise Ellwood; Elaine Chester; and George Welch, who only a couple of years later was my captain in Brothers A grade cricket side and principal of his own accountancy business in the city.

There was also our much-loved English teacher, Ada Walker, who was a student there in 1919 before teaching from 1924-52. Ex-students thought so highly of Miss Walker, who left teaching to run the Korner Shop Newsagency (Shields St) and later Walker's Book Shop (Lake St) with her brother Reg, that they held a celebration luncheon decades later in the 1980s for her birthday. I have fond memories of Miss Walker's lessons, especially how she encouraged lively

debate when we reviewed the books she set us to read. I loved playing the devil's advocate and recall how I argued (to her delight) that Shylock was justified in demanding his pound of flesh in *The Merchant of Venice*. "A deal's a deal" was my basic argument. I saw Miss Walker frequently in the city in later years. Usually we merely nodded or simply said "hello". While it may have been my imagination, I often felt she was looking at me with bemusement and no little wonder how the gangly kid who used to debate so fiercely with her about Shylock was now the editor of the city's daily newspaper.

I enjoyed my two years at Cairns High which passed fairly uneventfully, apart from a severe bout of dengue fever early in 1946 that disrupted my education. I always loved school but was feeling so ill one morning I cried off going, so my Mum said, "OK, let's get you up to the (Cairns Base) hospital." But no ambulance, taxi or public transport for us in those days: we walked all the way from 169 Bunda St. I was given a ticket with a number at the outpatients department and we waited our turn to see a doctor.

The last I remembered was standing in a queue, then waking up in a hospital bed. I spent a couple of weeks there, often quite delirious I was later told, and some time later convalescing at home. My mates called by with news of all the doings at Cairns High as they sat by my verandah bed. Even back at school, I was restricted in activities and could not play games or attend school parades for many weeks. Even the grumpiest of teachers were kind to me. I did not realise how ill I had been.

I finished my formal education at Year 10 level late in 1946 when I passed the State Junior Public Examination with better than average results. Some classmates continued on for two more years at Cairns High with a view to becoming teachers. A few went on to university, a rare achievement in those days for my social class. I would have liked to have gone on and in fact had been awarded a teacher training scholarship, which would have provided a little financial assistance. But by then my father had left the family home and I had to contribute to our meagre household budget. Or at least I could provide for my own upkeep, even though the most I could hope to earn was under £3 (about $180 today) a week.

In December 1946, it was time to launch myself into my working life. But doing what? Job-searching then was nothing like today: no supermarkets or the plethora of franchise stores and fast-food outlets for holiday jobs or as a start in a permanent position. Those classmates with modest academic achievement found jobs as apprentices in the butchering, motor and building trades, or took on more manual jobs as hands at local sawmills. But what were my prospects? The only experience I had was working part-time during school holidays. My first real job was offsider on Ernie Crane's milk run from his home in Draper St, near the Fiveways in Parramatta Park, when I was aged about 11. But I did not last long after I began nodding off in classes at

school and then the warmth of my bed on cooler mornings became too seductive.

I had earlier picked up a shilling or two during holidays at a bakery at 134 Sheridan St where my brother Fred was employed as an apprentice baker by Roy and Wallace Browne. The shopfront still stands today as Billabong Car Hire. Buildings down a laneway used to house the bakery at the rear and stables for horses that hauled the bread carts on the daily home delivery runs. My main job was to grease bread tins with a piece of hessian dipped into a pail of fat and paint a glaze on fruit buns with a brush dipped into a sugary liquid. In later school holidays, I had been a rouseabout at a car-wrecking yard, labourer in a sawmill yard and office boy at F.R. Ireland's motor dealership in Lake St.

I did not fancy a career as a milko, baker, car wrecker or saw miller. Well, according *The Cairns Post's* jobs section, Hughes & Laycock (Maranoa St) would teach a lad the glass trade, Northern Builders Supplies (Dutton St) had vacancies for two apprentice plumbers, Cairns City Council advertised for an apprentice motor mechanic, and Cairns Regional Electricity Board invited applications for electrical apprentices, aged 15-17 with a Scholarship Examination pass essential. Cummins & Campbell (Spence St), where I was to work 10 years later as a trainee salesman, had an opening for a junior male clerk, Crossland Motors (Lake St) wanted an "intelligent lad" for its workshop office, and F.R. Ireland's (Lake St) wanted a boy for messages. The OK Cash Store (McLeod St) had a job for a "strong, intelligent lad, 16-18 years for grocery trade", and H.M. Svendsen (Lake St) offered a trade in mattress-making.

Two positions that caught my eye were vacancies for a junior clerk at Chandlers and Mulgrave Shire Council. The first response I had to my written applications came from Chandlers. I was invited by letter for an interview at their store, then in Spence St next to the Cummins & Campbell building where Korean and Japanese restaurants operate today. I reported to manager Fred Leate, a kindly and considerate gentleman who surprised me at the end of the interview by saying, "Well, young Hudson, you can have the job if you like, but there'll not be much of a future for you here and I think someone with your ability can find something better for yourself in life."

Thankfully, I took Mr Leate at his word. A few days later, I was overjoyed to receive a letter from Mulgrave shire clerk Cecil de Graaf Williams telling me I had been appointed, without an interview, to the position of junior clerk at their offices at 51 The Esplanade, a building that today houses Tourism Tropical North Queensland. I did not learn until many years later that the money for that building came from the sale of the first standard gauge railway built and operated by a local authority. Profit from the sale of the Cairns-Mulgrave Tramway (about $2.7 million in today's dollars)

was used to build the offices. The tramway, which ran from Cairns to Babinda, was built and operated (profitably) by the Cairns Divisional Board, forerunner of the Cairns City Council, from 1897 until the Queensland government bought it in 1912. The tramway's terminus was across the road from today's Cape York Hotel. It was named the Tramway when it was built in 1898, became the National in 1926, and was renamed Cape York in 1987.

My first day at work at Mulgrave Shire Council, that Monday in January 1946, consisted of meeting my co-workers, including officer manager Hugh Henderson. Hugh was fond of telling people in later years that we had similar career paths: he started work as office boy at *The Cairns Post* and retired years later at Mulgrave Shire Council, whereas I

Prompt Printery in Lake St was one of the many family-owned businesses operating in Cairns in early post-World War II days. It was owned by the Collis family for more than 70 years. Dick Fry, who returned from WWII service to start his own business of NQEA, which became one of Australia's biggest engineering firms, worked there from the 1930s.

The Cairns (later Mulgrave) Shire offices at 51 Esplanade, circa 1930s, where Alan Hudson started his first job in January 1947. The building was vacated by the Mulgrave Shire Council in 1995 after the amalgamation with the Cairns City Council. It is now occupied by Tourism Tropical North Queensland.

started as office boy at the council and ended my working life as editor of the *Post*.

My duties, which seem so mundane today, sent my head spinning as they were explained: collect mail every morning from the post office on the corner of Abbott and Spence streets, take outgoing mail to the post office after recording every letter in a book, buy morning and afternoon teas for office staff and for council meetings from Cominos Cafe in Abbott St (where Orchid Plaza is today), run assorted messages around the town as directed, often to obtain signatures on cheques and documents.

Once a month, I spent the whole day riding the office bike around town with a port full of cheques, paying council's

monthly accounts. It was also my job to operate the Gestetner duplicating machine, running off mountains of meeting agendas and other office documents every day, usually getting my hands (and often my clothes) ink-stained.

When I was in the office, I sat at a small desk where the tiny manual switchboard was installed and I had to answer incoming calls. I learned the patter so well that my mother at breakfast one morning told me that the previous night I had woken the Hudson household, and probably half the neighbourhood. I had apparently bellowed out on several occasions in my sleep, "Mulgrave Shire, can I help you?" My working life, which was to take some interesting twists and turns over the next 20 years, was under way.

On September 13, 1947, Cairns people were given a stark and tragic reminder of the dangers of World War II when three seamen died and 25 were severely injured when the corvette HMAS Warrnambool sank within minutes of hitting a mine off Cape Grenville, more than 400km north of the city. Around 4pm that Saturday, a division of the mine-sweeping flotilla was hard at work, a group of corvettes trailing the larger sloop, HMAS Swan, along the jagged edge of Cockburn Reef. Whether Swan snagged a coral obstruction, or fouled on a mine, her cable float dipped and her sweep cable snapped. Warrnambool's response was to swing hard starboard, tucking in behind Swan. Her winch crew fully expected to snag on the same obstruction. Instead they struck a mine.

Of about 90 men aboard, many were in the mess, directly above where the mine hit. Those below the waterline, in and around the engine room, took a brunt of the blast. One of the stokers was fatally injured when lockers tore free and crushed his chest. Men in the heads were badly injured, slamming up into the deck head before crashing back down to smash the porcelain toilet bowls. Those on deck were lifted metres into the air as the bow section was lifted completely out of the water. From the bridge, the officer of the watch was blown through the glass and up toward the bow. A signalman was thrown from the bridge into the sea and disappeared.

Leading stoker E. Clark and stoker J. McBride were on duty in the boiler room at the time. With no consideration for their own safety, the two young men refused to leave their posts as the room filled with steam from bursting pipes and gushing fuel oil, until they managed to shut off the oil feed to furnaces. Officers later said the heroic action by Clark and McBride prevented a blaze that would have spread and blown up the boilers. It may well have killed every one of the 90 people on board.

I was among an estimated crowd of 8000 people who crammed into the Cairns waterfront area one Friday night in May 1948 to farewell one of the city's favourite visitors, the cruise liner Manunda. The ship was making its first call into Cairns since 1940 when the regular service had been curtailed because of the war.

The naming of Cairns suburbs as Manunda, Manoora and Kanimbla provides a permanent reminder of the days when shipping was the only means of transport between Cairns and the outside world. These steamers, together with several others, provided a weekly cargo and passenger service from southern ports. They brought cargo and a few hundred passengers at a time from southern capitals to Cairns for holidays in the district, most of them on a weekly run from Melbourne that called into Sydney, Brisbane and Townsville. Until Cairns was connected to Brisbane by rail in 1924 and commercial air services began in the early 1930s, we were entirely dependent on the service from these coastal steamers.

It was Manoora and Manunda that I remember most fondly for they were on the Melbourne-Cairns run when I was a schoolboy in the late 1930s, spending hours of my leisure time every week on the waterfront. I doubt there was a single occasion they were in port that I was not down at the wharves looking them over and dreaming how one day I'd be able to take a trip on them, which I never managed to achieve. My older brother Bill and I would run home from school, drop our bags into our place in Bunda St, and arrive at the main wharves, breathless, at around 4pm, just in time to see the ships moving away at the start of their voyage south. Their departure was always a grand occasion for the city. Huge crowds of locals would be there to see them off, throwing streamers to passengers, with one of the city's brass bands playing for more than an hour before departure.

These ships would be dwarfed by the ocean-going luxury liners of today, but I thought they were so awesome in their size (a report in a newspaper at the time described the Manoora, at 10,160 tonnes, as the "Monster of the Deep"). Manoora, named after the South Australian town of the same name meaning "a spring of water", was described as the finest vessel of her size and class that had ever been built on the River Clyde in Scotland. It had a special sports deck, a huge

Passengers disembark at Cairns in 1942 from the SS Ormiston, one of the coastal steamers that serviced the Melbourne-Cairns route for many years. Police wearing khaki uniforms of the time were on hand as an escort for Premier Forgan Smith who travelled on the vessel from Brisbane for an official visit to Cairns.

promenade deck of 70m, a large lounge enclosed by glass that doubled as a ballroom at night, with lifts and stairways between the six decks. It cruised at a little more than 18 knots. Manunda was smaller at 9144 tonnes. It was also built in Glasgow and arrived in Australia in May 1929.

These coastal steamers operated on the Melbourne-Fremantle run in the summer months and the Melbourne-Cairns service in the May-September period which we regarded for many years as our tourist "season". The reason we had a "season" for tourism was that there was a general attitude in North Queensland during my younger days that our southern cousins would not fancy coming up here in summer to endure the heat and humidity, the waves of disease-carrying mosquitoes, and run the risk of being swept away by floods and cyclones.

Many businesses generally planned their operations for a lull in trading during summer and I recall that Cummins & Campbell, the firm I worked for as a young man, would only order Hoadley's chocolates from Melbourne, including the famous Violet Crumble Bars, from April to October for fear they would wither away on the shelves of local shops in our summer heat. There was always an air of buoyancy about during the May-September period, and not only because it was the tourist season. The increase in tourist traffic coincided with the crushing season in the sugar industry, a time when at least 5000 extra jobs were created among the eight mill areas in the Far North in the days before computers and mechanisation did away with the need for manual canecutters and cut mill workforces by half.

The arrival of these steamers in our winter provided a

bonanza for local business houses, particularly the city hotels, taxis and transport services like the WhiteCar company. Passengers on the round trip had only three days in Cairns to see the sights. Some would take the rail trip to Kuranda and stay for a night or two at Fitzpatrick's Hotel. Other passengers took the WhiteCar service up the Gillies Highway and toured the Tablelands while staying at Jack Hanrahan's Malanda Hotel, with the Nasser family at their Barron Valley Hotel in Atherton, or at Maud Kehoe's Lake Eacham Hotel at Yungaburra.

A Perth businessman told *The Cairns Post* in May 1948: "We particularly like Yungaburra, and the lakes were beautiful. I've decided that one needs more than three days to see the north. Our whole stay here was a race against time." Several passengers chartered an aircraft and flew over the Tablelands. Taxi drivers had an arrangement with some city hotels that they would take five passengers on day trips around the district to such places as Innisfail where they would see a sugar mill in operation, and other attractions

like Paronella Park and Etty Bay. The taxis usually charged their passengers 10 shillings each at a time when the average weekly wage was less than five pounds (about $340).

When World War II brought a halt to the service, Manoora was converted to an armed merchant vessel for coastal duties, while Manunda became a hospital ship in May 1940. Manunda saw duty in the Middle East and the Pacific. It was in Darwin harbour with more than 40 other vessels when the Japanese bombed the city in February 1942. Manunda made more than 40 voyages during the war, transporting 30,000 service personnel, and brought many of the prisoners of war back to Australia at the end of the war in 1945.

When Manunda made her first trip back after the war on May 19, 1948, Cairns people gave it a tremendous welcome. A dance held at the Trocadero that night, with George Stone's orchestra playing, was advertised as the "biggest night Cairns has ever seen" and people flocked to the evening in their hundreds. But it was the farewell that was so amazing. With Cairns's population then below the 20,000 mark, more than

Bob (later Sir Robert) Norman, after his discharge from the RAAF, started his first business in Cairns in 1946 with brother Ron as Perfection Dry Cleaners at 75-79 Grafton St. The street then still had its brothels and seedy reputation and Bob Norman later recalled that PDC's business did not take off until police began moving the prostitutes out. Several illegal SP betting shops operated there at the time.

Billy Collins, Cairns's longest serving mayor, 1927-49, and wife Monica. Collins was mayor when three major projects were undertaken in Cairns: establishment of the Barron Falls Hydro-Electric Scheme, the start of the Cairns Mulgrave Water Supply Board and construction of the new council chambers in Abbott St.

8000 packed on to the main wharves on the night of Friday, May 21, 1948, to witness her departure at 8pm. The decks of Manunda were crowded with more than 300 passengers clutching at a continuous flow of colourful streamers, with the Cairns Municipal Band providing entertainment in the lead-up to her departure. Few Cairns people that night would have dreamed that the days of the coastal steamers were numbered. When the Adelaide Steamship Company found it could not operate both ships at a profit, due to increased competition from better and faster commercial air services, it sold Manunda to Japan in 1956. It became the Hakone Maru which was broken up in 1957. Manoora continued in the coastal service until 1961 but, after it completed a round trip from Sydney to Cairns, it was sold to the Indonesian government on August 9, 1961. The coastal steamer service was officially withdrawn in 1962.

Cairns had been predominantly a blue-collar electorate that favoured the Labor Party, but voters had supported the conservative William Aloysius (Billy) Collins to a record term as mayor of 22 years from April 1927. However, in 1949 they shocked Collins by turfing him out of office for Labor's candidate W.H. (Bill) Murchinson, a railway worker. Collins was a pharmacist (we called them chemists in those days) with a shop on the corner of Lake and Shields streets, where Qantas has had its offices in recent years.

Collins installed the first neon sign in Cairns in the late 1930s and "Collins Chemist" shone brightly over the city every night, facing Lake St to the south. It was beneath a tall radio tower on top of the building that provided transmission for the ABC which once had its studios on the top floor. I remember Collins as a kindly man, grey-haired, softly spoken, with a chubby face and a ready smile.

Collins was mayor when three major projects were undertaken in Cairns: establishment of the Barron Falls Hydro-Electric Scheme, the start of the Cairns Mulgrave Water Supply Board (CMWSB), and construction of the new council chambers in Abbott St. He was chairman of the Barron Falls scheme when it began operating in November 1935, and was the first chairman when it became the Cairns Regional Electricity Board on April 1, 1946. He was also the first chairman of the CMWSB in 1946. Cairns had drawn its first piped water supply from a reservoir at Freshwater Creek

POPULATION

Cairns population since 1900 (totals are approximate)

1900	–	4000
1905	–	3600
1910	–	5000
1915	–	5000
1920	–	6000
1925	–	8500
1930	–	9500
1935	–	13,000
1940	–	15,200
1945	–	15,000
1950	–	18,000
1955	–	21,400
1960	–	24,180
1965	–	26,500
1970	–	31,000
1975	–	35,500
1980	–	38,500
1985	–	39,700
1990	–	43,000
1995*	–	107,499
2000	–	117,066
2005	–	128,666
2021**	–	187,565

* Cairns City merged with Mulgrave Shire

** Based on 2 per cent annual average growth rate

in August 1911, and the CMWSB under his leadership began planning the Behana Creek scheme that first supplied water to Gordonvale in 1952, and Cairns a few years later.

Collins also organised a loan of £15,000 (about $1.2 million today) from the State government during the depression years to build the new council chambers, a building that now houses the city library. A large gathering celebrated the opening with a dinner in the new building on August 11, 1930. Collins was born at Herberton in 1886 and completed his education at Nudgee College, Brisbane, in 1904 by delivering the breaking-up oration which he titled *The Land of My Forefathers*, a tribute to his Irish heritage. Collins married Monica O'Callaghan. They lived for most of their married life on a spectacular hillside home at Edge Hill that they named "Sylvanbrook".

Apart from his work and his family, Collins's interests included the church, sailing, cricket and brass bands. He once owned an 18ft skiff, Sylvania, which he raced in Cairns Aquatic Club events in the years soon after World War I. Collins sold his pharmacy business in the mid-1950s to Archie Shaw. When he died on June 29, 1959, aged 71, hundreds attended what was believed to have been the city's first civic funeral as testimony to a man who was much loved and respected by local citizens.

As an indication that the pace of life in Cairns began stepping up a notch or two towards the end of the 1940s, a Sydney travel agency advertised in *The Cairns Post* that one could then travel by air "without delays" from Rome through Athens to Sydney "in only eight days". Use of motor vehicles in the city was becoming so prolific that the Cairns City Council considered whether parking should be allowed in the middle of the road in Shields St, between Grafton and Sheridan streets. Garden plots and trees in the locality could be "adjusted" to accommodate parking, a council committee recommended. However, police advised that because of the heavy traffic in Shields St and the presence of the trees and garden plots, parking of vehicles there would create too great a danger to other road users.

MOMENTS IN TIME

1942 – February 27
Government calls for voluntary evacuation of Cairns district due to threat of Japanese invasion and closes most Far North Queensland schools.

1942 – June 15
Highway to Tablelands via Smithfield and Kuranda opens.

1945 – March 5
RAAF Hudson Lockheed carrying top

defence personnel crashes into the sea off Machans Beach, killing all 23 on board.

1945 – August 15
Cairns celebrates end of World War II with official street procession.

1946 – March 29
Cairns Aero Club is formed.

1948 – October 4
First match played at Griffiths Park, Cairns

cricket's new headquarters.

1949 – May 28
W.A. (Billy) Collins, city's longest serving mayor (1927-49) is defeated by Labor candidate W.H. (Bill) Murchison.

1949 – August 28
Francis Richard Holland, 34, dies after shark attack at Yorkeys Knob.

The low level bridge and approaches over the Barron River near Kuranda were widened by the Allied Works Council in the early part of World War II. The original bridge designed specifically for motor traffic over the Barron was built around 1926. A new bridge replaced it in 1938. The present bridge, about 275m above the river, was built in the early 1960s.

Broad brush strokes of the professional ticket writer display the weekly grocery specials at Manahans, one of the four grocery stores in Lake St with Brightways, Armstrong Ledlie & Stillman and Bolands before the major chains moved into Cairns in the 1960s. From left: Norma Roberts (cashier), Arthur Nicholls, Arthur Keller, Les Horn (manager) and Frank Allen-Aitkens.

CHAPTER THREE - 1950s

s life in Cairns moved into the 1950s, most of the city's streets were still unpaved. Former city engineer Graeme Haussmann once told me that when he arrived here to join the Cairns City Council in mid-1954, only 33km of the 166km of roads within its boundaries were sealed with bitumen. But it was to be an eventful decade with the first cyclone I have experienced hitting Cairns, the introduction of television, the Olympic Games held in Australia for the first time, and hundreds of European migrants welcomed to this city.

The "golden block", bounded by Spence, Abbott, Shields and Lake streets was the hub of business activity. It was a leisurely time for the laidback locals whose social life revolved around dances at the Aquatic (Wharf St) and Trocadero (Shields St and later Grafton St), musicals and other events at the Hibernian Hall (Florence St), and the pictures (movies) at two city theatres, Tropical (Abbott St) and Palace (Lake St), and the two suburbans, Plaza (Mulgrave Rd) and Rex (Sheridan St).

Teenagers of that time did not space themselves out on illegal drugs and binge drinking at pubs and nightclubs, nor gate-crash private celebrations or attend rave parties in their hundreds. They found no need to arm themselves with knives and other weapons for the drunken weekend punch-up, take part in street brawls or attack innocent passers-by. None of my friends had a car and those few I knew who had them did not amuse themselves by hooning around the streets at night. It must seem to youngsters of today that we were a boring lot.

My mates and I, all members of Brothers footy club, were typical of teens of that time. We did not drink alcohol to

Dancing at the Aquatic on the Esplanade was one of the most popular social outings in Cairns in the 1940s-50s.

Marion Jenkins and her band of Frank Smith, Dick Bolton and Jack Bolton (drums), playing at a dinner dance at the Central Hotel, circa 1940. Marion's band played at local dances, mainly the Aquatic, from the time she formed her band at the age of 17. Jack Frousicker and Larry O'Connell were other members of the band. Marion and her husband Allan Amos, whom she married in 1944, in later years played at many social club events at places like West Cairns Bowls Club. Their last engagement was a function at the Mallon home at Smithfield in the 1980s.

get our kicks. Twice a week during our two under-20 footy seasons, we attended the Winkworth St home of our coach Jack Brown and his wife Dorrie where we played cards, enjoyed music, chatted away and ended the evening with a great feast of sandwiches, cakes and cups of tea. On the other nights of the week, we went to the pictures or a dance, played snooker one night at Crowley's billiard room in Shields St, and held a card-playing evening at Col Wales's home in Terminus St. We usually ended our evenings in town with a milkshake and toasted sandwiches at the Beehive Cafe below what is today's Cairns Museum in the City Place. On Sundays during the summer, we rode our bikes for a day's outing to one of the district's favoured picnic spots, mainly Lake Placid or Yorkeys Knob. We all enjoyed a beer but none us drank regularly until we were into our 20s. But I am sure most of my contemporaries would agree that our youth was a time of great fun when we enjoyed ourselves immensely.

Window-shopping, a pastime that has long been forgotten by most people, provided Cairns families with hours of enjoyment, and locals spent many of their evenings strolling around the "golden block" to enjoy the window displays which were changed every so often to coincide with special events such as Easter, the Cairns Show and Christmas.

Window-dressing and ticket-writing were an art form and many stores employed their own display artists. Major retailers in Bolands, Harris Brothers, R.H. Kellys, Mazlins, C.R. Smith & Co, Mrs Carr's Paris House and A.J. Drapers, and many smaller outlets, entered into a friendly competition to try to outdo one another. And not only the clothing, footwear and jewellery stores had eye-catching window exhibits but also confectionery displays. The array of cakes at places like Wilesmiths (Lake St) and even windows of fish vendors drew attention.

The CBD's five major grocery stores usually painted their specials for the week prominently on their windows. In later years, most of the city's retailers and business houses dressed their premises in tropical themes for the annual Fun in the Sun Festival competition.

An annual window-dressing competition used to be held in Cairns. Smithy Holmes, a professional display artist, was Harris Brothers' Innisfail store manager who came to Cairns in the 1950s to judge the contest. Eddie Halford dressed the windows for R.H. Kellys (Abbott St). I always regard Bert Crease as being the doyen of the local window-dressers. Bert came from England as a 20-year-old, working first for Rothwells in Brisbane before coming north in 1937 to join Nolans at Innisfail. He came to Cairns when he was offered a job at A.J. Drapers in 1940 and then worked in turn for

Mazlins, Bolands, for many years with Crofton Clauson and, until he retired, as a salesman for *The Cairns Post*. Stewart Heilbron was the display artist at Bolands around the early 1950s, followed later by Terry Brophy and his wife, Liz, a talented painter whose work was often exhibited locally. Window displays for C.R. Smith & Co, a menswear store in Lake St and later Abbott St, were usually done by sales staff like Danny Curtin, Sid Harvey and Frank Goldfinch.

Families and courting couples often spent early evenings, particularly at weekends, strolling around the "golden block" and window shopping, stopping to yarn with friends, and enjoying a recital by one of the city's brass bands. If an

John Lizzio was one of several old-style barbers who had shops in the CBD. He had a shop at 78 Shields St from 1945. He was popular with the kids because he cut their hair while they sat on a toy horse. He built a house at 253 Mulgrave Rd and transferred his business there in 1964 and continued cutting hair there until he died in 1994. The barber shop is still there. Other popular city barbers at the time were Bert Butler, Tom Cowles and Bill Bragg.

election was in the offing, candidates spruiked their promises to voters from the back of a truck outside Fostars Shoes store in Shields St. Most CBD businesses then were long-established and family owned, their proprietors known to locals by their first names. Most have passed on, but older locals reflecting on the early days of Cairns recall this time as among their fondest memories. It certainly was mine. Couples looked at engagement rings in the windows of jewellers Tom McDonald (Abbott St), Crofton Clauson (Shields St) and Ronalds (Spence St), or bridal wear in Mrs Carr's Paris House in Lake St.

Dick Van Dorssen, whose son Lionel later took over the shop and became the city's deputy mayor, usually kept open to accommodate the strollers at his tobacconist and barber shop in Abbott St next to the Court House Hotel, and then there was A.J. Drapers auctioneer and furniture store (where our future mayor Ron Davis worked), Kodak, men's and women's clothing outlets of R.H. Kelly and Harris Brothers. In Shields St, there were Adairs Silk Store, Pioneer Tours, O'Connells newsagents, Ted Fisk's Bookstore, Fostars Shoes

(managed for many years by Harry Mackenroth), Clausons, Black and White Cafe and Mazlin's Corner.

Evening strollers would have a milkshake or ice-cream soda at the Blue Bird Cafe (corner of Abbott and Shields), an orange drink at the Palace Theatre (Lake St) refreshment bar run by the Diakos family, or buy a packet of freshly salted peanuts from Mick and Bill Condullas at the Black and White Cafe. Jim Botsolos ("Barramundi Jim") was usually standing outside his New City Cafe (Lake St), and further along were Prompt Printery owned by Tom Collis, the pharmacy run by Chas Herries, Sydney H. Turner's electrical store, Lionel Law's Chargois Studio's display window with the latest wedding photos, then next door to Angelo and George Thimios' Central Cafe. Wilesmith's cake and a coffee shop came next, then Koch and Lazarus shoe repairers, Rod Absell's newsagency, the Gas Supply Co, Bill and Steve Thimios' clothing store and Boland's grocery department.

A tour of the block would be completed with a look in every display in Boland's windows in Spence St down to the tailor shop run by Dave Muirhead and son Johnny, on

Dick Van Dorssen behind the counter at his shop at 99 Abbott St, where Orchid Plaza is today, with assistant Joan Bradford (later Mrs Noel Holding). Van Dorssen was a barber and tobacconist, who opened his business in early evenings in pre-television days, which old-timers remember fondly as a time when a stroll around the main city block was the social highlight of the week.

Cominos Cafe in Abbott St, where Orchid Plaza is today, was the grandest in Cairns from the time it opened in 1926 until its closure in 1952. It was the biggest and most popular of the places for meals and takeaway sandwiches, cakes and other snacks. George Cominos was a man before his time, basing his successful business on quality and service. The public could use the cafe's rest rooms with showers and "powder room" at no charge, and telephone booths and writing cubicles with free stationery were available. Mr Cominos had grand plans for expansion, but World War II intervened in his proposal to introduce a roof garden for dancing and other recreational activities, a free kindergarten for use by shoppers, introduction of a superannuation scheme, and construction of a holiday resort for staff, family and friends.

to Ronalds' jewellers and around the Abbott St corner to the pharmacy owned by George Covacevich and later by Ralph Tobiano, Paling's music and sports store operated by Charlie Dawson, then Whittick's newsagency and Wal Balzer's pharmacy, on to Tom McDonald's jewellers and finally to the grand cafe owned by George Cominos.

It was inconceivable in the 1950s to people of my generation that these, and other CBD businesses, would not always be a part of our lives. We grew up with them. They were almost an institution. Even now I cannot get out of the habit of referring to the Rockmans building on City Place as "Mazlin's Corner", even though the Mazlin family

sold it 50 years ago. Dining out in the 1950s at some of these CBD outlets was a world the present generation would not recognise: no McDonalds, no Subway, no Kentucky Fried, no Chinese or sushi bars, no fast food outlets of any kind, no licensed restaurants, and pubs did not start to serve counter meals until at least the 1960s.

Office workers, shop assistants and businessmen had their lunches at their favourite CBD cafe, or bought sandwiches and fish chips to take away. Some ate their lunches in the spacious Anzac Park, where the Reef Casino is now.

Cominos Cafe in Abbott St, where Orchid Plaza is today, was the biggest and most popular of the places in town for meals and takeaway sandwiches, cakes and other

Commuters to Cairns from as far away as Mareeba and Tully once travelled to the centre on regular railmotor services. The service out of Cairns was at its peak in the 1930s when it provided more than 30 journeys a week carrying up to 175 passengers at a time. But it was still popular into the 1950s. Regulars included office workers and shop assistants, people going to town for a day's shopping or to an afternoon movie, and students attending the Cairns high schools before secondary schools opened in Gordonvale in 1965 and later in other outlying suburbs. The Aloomba-Cairns service, with more than 20 stops, took up to an hour. A few waterside workers regularly used it, and the railmotor continued through to Wharf St to drop them off at the main wharf gates. Bill Murchison, mayor of Cairns (1949-52), and Ray Jones, a city alderman (1962-66) and State Labor member for Cairns (1965-83), were once porters on the railmotor service out of Cairns.

snacks. It was opened by George Cominos in 1926 after he had started his first store in Cairns in 1906. Cominos was a man before his time, basing his successful business on quality and service. The public could use the cafe's rest rooms with showers and "powder room" at no charge, and telephone booths and writing cubicles with free stationery were available. Cominos had grand plans for expansion, but World War II intervened in his proposal to introduce a roof garden for dancing and other recreational activities, a free kindergarten for use by shoppers, introduction of a superannuation scheme, and construction of a holiday resort

for staff, family and friends. The cafe was often host to outside broadcasts by Radio 4CA in the 1940s.

I often treated myself to an ice cream soda there, and one of my jobs when I was office boy at Mulgrave Shire Council on the Esplanade in 1947-48 was to take orders from staff for the morning teas and lunches I would buy there. A team of girls made up sandwiches and rolls behind a counter at the rear of the cafe, and one of the favourites of the Mulgrave staff was apple turnovers, one of the more expensive morning tea items at sixpence each. Girls from the offices of solicitors, accountants and state government buildings in Abbott St would take a cup or a small container to the cafe and buy a penny's worth of milk for morning tea, and often a few twirls of butter for their buns and rolls. Closure of the cafe in 1952 was a great shock to locals, but George Cominos' health was failing and his sons George and Peter were pursuing other careers. My good friend Peter Cominos in recent times was still hosting regular get-togethers of former cafe staff, more than half a century after it closed.

The Victory Cafe was another CBD institution which stood the test of time through to recent years. Specialising in fish and chip meals and takeaways, the Victory began its life in Shields St near Hides Hotel in the 1940s when Andrew Kazamias had it. Andrew moved it when new shops were being built there in the early 1950s to the premises at 68 Shields St where Bill Fulton – later mayor of Cairns, then Member for Leichhardt – ran his bicycle and sports goods shop. Helen and Peter Milaras bought the Victory from Angelo and George Thimios who had it from 1960-69. They ran the Victory from 1969 until they retired in 1994.

I met the Thimios brothers when they had the Central Cafe, near the Lake St entrance to today's Orchid Plaza. Their father Steve started the business in the early 1930s. They were forced to move in 1958 when Coles took over Penneys and extended the store from Abbott through to Lake St. The Koola Cafe and Milk Bar also operated in Abbott St in the post-World War II years in the Great Northern Hotel building opposite *The Cairns Post* offices. Other popular CBD cafes in those years were the Blue Bird, corner Abbott and Shields, Golden Vale in Shields St near the Lake St corner, Black & White, opposite the Golden Vale, and Jim Botsolos's New City, which specialised in fish and steak meals, and the Beehive Cafe, below today's Cairns Museum on City Place.

Nightlife in Cairns in the 1950s came to an abrupt halt after the pictures came out at 11pm and dances finished at the Trocadero or the Aquatic on Friday or Saturday just on midnight. The lights of Cairns went out and the CBD resembled a ghost town. One exception was

on Friday nights when a mobile diner was parked in Abbott St outside the Tropical Theatre serving a basic meal of pies, boiled savelofs, peas and potato, served with coffee or tea. They did a roaring trade, especially with men who put a dent in their pay packet during extended drinking sessions across the road at the Imperial Hotel and other city pubs.

Another popular outlet emerged in the early 1950s when an enterprising fellow named Roy Delaforce opened a milk bar on the corner of Aplin and McLeod streets, opposite the Queens Hotel where I was boarding. He traded as late into the night as there was a demand for his services. Roy, a short, unassuming fellow who padded around behind the counter in bare feet most of the time, sold fish and chips, soft drinks, other snacks and refreshments.

I can testify that his milkshakes were the best in town. "See you at Roy's" became a catchcry among young Cairns people. They congregated there in numbers after their night out. It was not unusual to find up to 50 or so there, some inside the shop and others spilling out on to the footpath until the wee hours of the morning. Roy later moved down Aplin St to larger premises at about No. 10 where he continued to enjoy the same success. Roy Delaforce was a trailblazer for Cairns. No one could have suspected in those early post-war years that a milk bar would succeed by doing the bulk of its business between 11pm and 2am.

But others soon followed Roy's lead and places like the Chick Bar, Rhonda's and Sally's in Grafton St, and Bill Gray's hamburger shop in Spence St, near the Grafton St intersection, became popular late-night stopovers with young people into the 1950s and beyond.

One of my favourites of those early years was the Red Oriental, another pioneer of late-night trading in Cairns. The Red Oriental, in Lake St opposite what later became the Playpen nightclub, was a decrepit old structure that I can only remember as always looking in need of repairs and a coat of paint. It was a two-storey building with a residence above and the cafe below catering for late-night prowlers looking for sustenance after the pubs had closed or for partygoers who

Ellis Beach resort was a popular destination in the 1960s when it, the Kowloon (Lake St) and Tropicana (Esplanade) were the first licensed restaurants in North Queensland. The proprietors Marge and Dave Fisher developed the Ellis Beach resort into one of the district's most popular dining-out venues with its licence to serve liquor with meals a novel attraction at the time.

had missed their evening meal. Sparsely furnished with tables with Formica tops and plastic chairs, its decor could only be described as understated (probably your 1940s Barbary Coast style) with the barest of adornment on walls whose colour, weathered by age and grime, defied description. Timmy Lau, proprietor, chef and waiter, worked away in his kitchen in full view of his patrons in an often boisterous environment, blithely ignoring the shouting and outrageous comment about the quality of his meals and standard of service.

No contemporary history of Cairns would be complete without an account of consumer and lifestyle habits that were introduced by outlets like Roy's, the Chick Bar, Rhonda's, Sally's and Bill Gray's that are taken for granted today. Early Chinese cafes, like the Red Oriental, were pioneers of the present takeaway phenomenon when, before those neat little plastic boxes were invented, customers brought their own container, maybe a dish or a saucepan, to take their meals away. Among other trail-blazers of dining-out around this time were Marge and Dave Fisher, who developed the Ellis

Beach Resort into one of the most popular dining-out venues for Cairns people. They had no hesitation in driving the return journey of 30 or so kilometres on Friday or Saturday night.

The Fishers and two other Cairns restaurants, the Kowloon in Lake St and the Tropicana on the Esplanade, about where Barnacle Bill's is now located, were the first three outlets to be granted liquor licences in North Queensland when the state government began relaxing its licensing laws in the early 1960s. The Ellis Beach venture became a real family affair for the Fishers with their sons Wally and Ray, and daughters Gay (later Mrs Don McDowall) and Dale (Mrs Ken Goopy) all working there. Marge and Dave Fisher took over Ellis Beach tearooms in the late 1950s when they provided little more than a brief half-way refreshment stop for motorists and the few tour buses travelling between Cairns. I am only one of hundreds of Cairns people who spent many an enjoyable outing at the Ellis Beach Resort, enjoying both the food and the music provided by groups like the Webb Trio, Eddie Owens and his Tempo Twisters and the Fireflies.

When my mother died in May 1951, I faced one of life's realities for the first time and had to fend for myself after years of being fed, clothed and generally mollycoddled. While singles these days share accommodation in houses or units, young people of my era boarded in private houses, at one of the 30 or more boarding houses in Cairns, or in one of several working class hotels. Single girls stayed either in private homes which let out one of their rooms to a boarder or at the Cairns branch of the Queensland Country Women's Association's Paulina McManus Memorial Home which was at 99 Esplanade from its early days in the 1930s until it was sold in the 1980s. It was previously Mrs Aumuller's boarding house, one of many along the seafront.

I stayed for a few weeks as a boarder in a home in Bungalow but the arrangement did not suit either party as I was working at night, and slept for much of the day. I then moved to Mrs Mary Gsell's boarding house in Taylor St, opposite the Cairns Brewery, where I shared a room with a friend, adjoining the dining room upstairs that seated 16 hungry men at meal-times. This part of Cairns was a heavily populated working class suburb with two sawmills, brewery, gasworks, the wharves where up to 1000 were employed, and the railways, all within a few hundred metres of one another. Around the corner from Mrs Gsell's in Spence St, the mothers of two of my footy mates, George Fitzpatrick and Joe Hickey, had boarding houses on opposite sides of the street. Mary Hickey came to Cairns in 1937 from Townsville and bought the Glasgow boarding house at 116 Spence St, which she renamed the Cairns Boarding House, and continued to operate it until well into the 1950s.

These boarding houses functioned under the proprietor's own, often quirky, set of rules which were necessary to ensure any semblance of orderly behaviour from a mishmash of male personalities. Unfortunately, my stay with Mrs Gsell, a member of the well-known Curtin family, lasted only a few months. I returned from overnight work one morning a little after 7am to find that I had been evicted. It transpired that my roommate, a modest drinker by any standards, had a couple too many at a celebration. During the night, he caused a commotion and aroused many sleeping occupants when he felt unwell and used the nearest window instead of the toilet.

The Norman Park boarding house, run by Marjorie Doman at 120 Sheridan St from 1945-54, was one of many in Cairns. It took its name from the adjacent park, now known as Munro Martin Park. It had about 15 rooms. Its main feature, a large poinciana tree in front of the building, was a magnificent sight when in bloom as it shaded much of the building. The boarding house accommodated an interesting collection of characters among the wharfies, meatworkers, sawmill hands and others who stayed there.

I was happy enough to share my roommate's fate, but I asked Mrs Gsell to explain the logic of her Irish justice to banish me from her establishment when I had been slaving away all night for the PMG (Post Master General) in the service of the district's telephone subscribers. She answered brusquely, "You're his mate, so you have to go, too." So move we did, to the Queens Hotel in McLeod St, run by Bill and Olive Allendorf on the corner opposite today's Cairns Central. I had a happy couple of years there at a weekly fee of £5/10/- (about $200 today), which was about half of my net wage, for three meals a day and a share room, in the company of several other office and blue-collar workers.

In the years soon after World War II, one could walk northwards down any of the main streets of Cairns, starting at Spence St, and find several boarding houses. Two of the oldest, the Shangrila on the corner of Spence and Grafton, and the original ambulance centre, corner Spence and Sheridan, continued to provide low budget accommodation until recent years. Ma Peel took in boarders in a two-storey building in Digger St, near the Grove St intersection, that may have previously been a private hospital. Cam Boyle, a friend who lived in Gordonvale but worked in Cairns, told me he stayed there when it cost 30 shillings (about $85 today) a week for accommodation and three meals a day.

A popular Esplanade boarding house was the Carlton at No. 129, a lovely old colonial-style home that was once the residence of Dr Edward Koch, one of the city's earliest doctors whose great work for the community was recognised by the dedication of a drinking fountain at the intersection of Abbott and Spence streets in 1903. Others were the Homeleigh at 173 Esplanade; Mrs Fuorro's on the corner of Aplin and the Esplanade, which was a girls' hostel; the Oakland Guest House at No. 105; and Hoole's, about where the RSL is now. Others in Lake St included the Rosedale, Kirkdale, Mabro and Auckland, and the former St Margaret's private hospital at 137 Lake, run as a boarding house by Mrs H. Burkitt. Others were the Allamba at 43 Grafton St, Lynton House at 54 Sheridan St and the Railway Guest House, 31

Sheridan St, and Millaa Millaa Guest House at 100 Sheridan St. The Norman Park boarding house at 120 Sheridan St was run from 1945-54 by Marjorie Doman, whose son Bill was a friend. Taking its name from the adjacent park, now known as Munro Martin Park, it had about 15 rooms and a flatette. Its main feature was a large poinciana tree in front that was a magnificent sight when in full bloom.

Like most of these old boarding houses, it accommodated an interesting collection of characters among the wharfies, meatworkers, sawmill hands and other workers, some of whom I knew. They included Jimmy Brown, a popular local events bookmaker; Fred Homan, a storeman at Burns Philp who was an opening bat for Rovers during my cricketing days; and Roy Delaforce, who opened Cairns's first late-night milk bar in Aplin St around 1950. Another boarder there was "Sinker" Simons, a billiard saloon keeper who was in charge of Crowley's billiard saloon in Shields St when my mates and I frequented the place in the late 1940s.

Bill Doman told me once that his mother was in the habit of stashing her takings in the old wood stove in the kitchen overnight. One night the oldest resident boarder, Pop McKay, had a headache and lit the fire to make himself a cup of tea, incinerating the fortnight's takings. The boarders took up a collection and compensated her for her loss.

I well recall the optimism in the city when an effort was made to restart local industry and establish a major outlet for district fruit crops with a canning factory. Production began in January 1951 at Smiths Creek at the end of Aumuller St in a former navy store with a floor space of 9200sq m. The Great Northern Cannery Co-operative Association Limited was registered on November 2, 1948. Nominal capital was set at £50,000 (about $2.6 million in today's values), divided into 50,000 ordinary shares of £1 (about $52) each.

By June 1949, some 8500 shares had been allocated to 143 members and, a year later, 179 farmer/shareholders held a total of 11,700 shares. It later transpired that it was never fully subscribed, and under-capitalisation would prove to

Up to 100 women worked at the Great North Cannery at Smith's Creek, Cairns, from the time it opened in May 1951 until it closed in 1957 because of continuing financial difficulties.

be a stumbling block for a venture that began with so much promise. The cannery was officially opened on December 21, 1950 by Minister for Agriculture Harold Collins, who had been convinced by growers of the viability of a cannery to process not only locally grown fruit, but possibly also vegetables and meat. Ernie Douglas, an experienced cannery engineer from Shepparton in Victoria, was appointed factory manager. The appointment of farmers as directors indicated the widespread area from where growers would send fruit to be canned: Walter Kelly (chairman) of Carbeen near Atherton; Dave Mason (Freshwater); M. Sheehan (Glen Boughton); R.E. Shepparson (Koah); D.S. Coleman (Yungaburra); F.B. Pulver (Atherton); I.H. Buchanan (East Palmerston); A.A. Mason (Cape Tribulation); and J. Martin (Daintree). Ernie Kerr, a partner in the Cairns firm of public accountants, Kerr Tadman & Co, was secretary.

Pineapples were an obvious first choice for processing.

They had been grown in Queensland since 1838 and, a century later, almost all of the pineapples in Australia came from this state. Although some historians record that Bowen and Magnetic Island pioneered the commercial growing of the fruit in North Queensland, pineapples were grown successfully in Cairns as far back as 1900. In the cannery's early years, a director, W.G. ("Banjo") Lazzarini, supervised the purchase of some two million pineapple plants from the Mary Valley in the Wide Bay area for Far North growers.

A competition was held for a trade name for the local product. About 1200 entries were received and Miss J. Cosgrove, of Abbott St, won 10 guineas (about $550) for her entry of "Amberglow" which was adopted. In the initial stages, the cannery processed mainly pineapples as sliced, pieces, crushed and juice, then papaws and passionfruit, and later mangoes, fruit salad, grapefruit juice, jams and chutney.

The cannery began producing orange juice in August 1951

from fruit grown in the Charters Towers and Cardwell areas. Markets for Amberglow products were established throughout Australia, New Zealand, Canada and the United Kingdom. A good friend, Thelma Perry, later to become Mrs Neil Joice, worked there in the mid-1950s during school holidays on the cannery's weighbridge, checking in the crates of pineapples from farms throughout the district. Thelma told me that up to 100 women – both locals and itinerants in the district – were employed, working two shifts to process the fruit.

It hit a crisis when the 1954 summer crop of pineapples was being picked. At the peak of the harvest, operations were suspended due to a lack of cans, cartons and labels. This resulted in 13,600 crates of fruit being dumped. The fruit had became over-ripe, for which growers had to be paid, and railing costs for another 550 cases for processing at the Northgate cannery in Brisbane. The cannery struggled from this point and its days were numbered as a local growers' co-operative. By December 1955, the Committee of Direction of Fruit Marketing (COD) had agreed to take over its outstanding debts. Manager Ernie Douglas resigned and COD appointed its own manager, and Cairns virtually became a branch of the COD's Northgate cannery. Although Cairns continued to operate through 1956-57, COD made no secret of its policy of centralisation at Northgate where its products were marketed under the brand name of Golden Circle.

It closed the Cairns plant at the end of the 1957 summer season and directed all fruit from the Far North must be sent to the COD cannery in Rockhampton. However, COD soon after closed Rockhampton and ordered that growers had to pay their own freight for fruit sent to Northgate.

This decision effectively killed pineapple growing for canning in Far North Queensland since the marketing costs were close to the amount paid by the cannery for fruit, with the added risk of no payment if fruit was considered not up to factory standard. Hundreds of growers, most of them cannery shareholders, lost thousands of dollars in the venture. After several attempts to revive it, the Smith's Creek cannery building was eventually demolished in the 1970s.

Conventional wisdom seems to be that environmental protests emerged in our society from the early 1980s with logging of Far Northern rainforests and the proposal for their World Heritage listing. However, 100 years earlier, the citizens of Cairns were outraged when, in the mid-1880s, Cairns Municipal Council decided it was time to remove a large fig tree in the courthouse grounds in Abbott St. Locals were outraged. It had been known as the "Tree of Knowledge" and was said to have been 700 years old. Bullock teamsters used to gather beneath it between their trips taking supplies to the rich mining regions of the hinterland.

Dr Edward Myers, who opened the first hospital in Cairns in 1876, and two other prominent local citizens, George Mackay and William Collinson, sat under the tree for two days and two nights armed with revolvers. They threatened to shoot anyone who tried to cut it down, but they revealed later that their guns were not loaded. Their protest worked. The council relented and gave the old tree a reprieve. But it was eventually cut down in 1920 after the original wooden courthouse building was levelled in 1919 to make way for a new building that was used for the first time in 1922.

The junior partner of the courthouse fig tree (Ficus infectoria), only a few metres away in Abbott St, caused even more of a public outcry when the Cairns City Council decided in July 1953 that it should be removed. Its roots had begun spreading and destabilising the foundations of nearby buildings and they had long since sprouted up in the roadway itself, cracking the bitumen surface. I was one of many local cyclists and motorists who detoured around the exposed roots as a matter of routine without giving it a second thought.

This tree, outside the former AMP and W. Smith & Co. buildings at 34-36 Abbott St, was one of the city's landmarks. A correspondent to *The Cairns Post* around this time wrote: "Tourists may not be greatly impressed with other features of the city, but most will surely remember the great tree when every other feature of this town will be forgotten."

However, the Cairns City Council was unimpressed by its heritage value and proceeded with plans to demolish

A well-loved city landmark was a giant fig tree in Abbott St (at left) which was cut down by Cairns City Council late in July 1953 despite strong opposition by locals.

it. Mayor Bill Fulton, who later represented the district as Labor's Federal Member for Leichhardt, defending allegations that he and his fellow aldermen were behaving like vandals, said the tree had no traditional or heritage significance. When successfully moving the motion on July 20, 1953 for the tree's demolition, Ald. G.W.G. (Watty) Wallace, the Bunda St butcher who went on to become the Labor Member for Cairns, wore a blue tie adorned with a hand-painted tree in full bloom. He laughed as he told his colleagues that the tie had been presented to him by a tree-lover after an earlier discussion about the fig tree's future. Citizens were angry. A save-the-tree committee was formed at a public meeting in a packed Hibernian Hall (corner Lake

and Florence streets) on July 27, 1953. Dr Hugo Flecker, the famed botanist after whom the Flecker Botanic Gardens were named, and Henry MacDonnell, principal partner and founder of the legal firm of that name, led a deputation to the council.

But they failed to change the decision. *The Cairns Post* suggested a poll of ratepayers on the issue, but the council refused. Axemen, supervised by timber industry veteran Bert Gane, moved in and began their unpopular task on Monday, July 20, 1953. I mingled at various times with the hundreds of locals who gathered on the eastern side of the street to witness the death throes of a tree most locals regarded as an old friend. At one time, a saxophonist entertained them with tunes appropriate to the moment, including *Trees, A Tree in the Meadow*, and *I Played My Love Song to a Tree*. By late afternoon, the old tree had its lower limbs hacked off to be taken away in council trucks. Work continued all week, then after a weekend respite, the coup de grace was delivered on Monday, August 4, 1953 when a council grader nudged the lower trunk and roots out of their centuries-old foundations. The last pieces were taken away on the back of a truck. Destruction of the landmark tree was a talking point in the city for a long time afterwards.

The 1950s were the time when Cairns welcomed hundreds of new settlers to the district. Some 170,000 Italians settled in Australia during that decade, as well as thousands of displaced persons from the war-ravaged Baltic states. Some ships carrying the new arrivals came directly to Cairns and I remember how civic leaders held a great welcome for them at the wharves after their ship berthed. Itala Imerito, who later moved from Harvey Creek, near Babinda, with her husband to live in Perth, became the first person to take out her citizenship at a public naturalisation ceremony at the Cairns City Council chambers on November 7, 1953 at the annual general meeting of the Queensland Country Women's Association.

Most new arrivals at Cairns were housed initially at the Migrant Centre in Hartley St, officially known as the Cairns Immigration Holding Centre, where accommodation was provided for about 450 people. Cairns was one of 24 similar centres set up throughout Australia. Some of the buildings were formerly US Army sheds, converted by the Department of Works and Housing and opened in August 1950. The Migrant Centre had several buildings on land over about 3ha, including four accommodation huts with separate ablution and laundry facilities, two staff blocks, mess and recreation halls, a kitchen and hospital, an administration office, and a supervisor's residence. The family of George Manier, who was a local taxi driver for 32 years, lived there for two years after they arrived in Melbourne in 1950 under the displaced persons migration scheme. George and his brother Andy cut

cane near Ingham where they had been sent under a bonding agreement they signed in Europe. The new arrivals were bonded to work in a nominated industry for at least two years, regardless of their previous employment experience. Some were academics who had never done manual work in their lives. The centre closed at the end of December 1952, reopened briefly in June 1953 to house wharf labourers who had transferred to Cairns from the south, then opened again to house migrants, mostly Italians, who arrived in Cairns on the Flaminia (1955), Aurelia (1956) and Toscana (1957).

One of the abandoned Migrant Centre buildings, built by the American Army during World War II, was bought at auction by the Cairns Little Theatre in 1963 for its first permanent home. The CLT previously staged its shows at the old Hibernian Hall, on the corner of Florence and Lake streets, and the Methodist Central Hall in Aplin St where it presented its first production on December 13, 1954. Kevin and Narelle Shorey, CLT stalwarts for many years, told me how in the 1950s they used a small building to store their equipment in the grounds now occupied by the Cairns Civic Theatre and staged rehearsals outside on the lawn.

The first production there in April 1965 was *Dial M for Murder*, directed by Charles Eustance. The Hartley St theatre became a busy place with 40 major plays being presented there. *A Man for All Seasons, Reedy River, Streetcar Named Desire, The One Day of The Year* and *Who's Afraid of Virginia Woolf* were just a small selection. These productions involved the likes of Reg Stocker, Charles Eustance, Eric Rees, Margaret Ramsay, Paul Day and Ted Kelk, only a few of the well-known and dedicated CLT members. It eventually became obvious CLT audiences wanted more modern venues so the group began performing in the Cairns Civic Theatre in June 1976 and the Hartley St building was sold in 1978 to kick-start the fundraising which built the Rondo Theatre in Greenslopes St. The Rondo opened its doors for the first production, *Female Parts*, in June 1983.

The Air Training Corps, which used one of the old Migrant Centre buildings for a short time in the 1950s, was formed on June 11, 1941 to provide pre-entry training for youths aged 16-18 who wanted to join the RAAF. During the war years, 14,000 young men graduated and went into RAAF. During the war, the Air Training Corps in Cairns was No.63 Squadron under Flight Lieutenant Fred Leate. The unit was disbanded at the end of the war but the exact date is unknown. The ATC was re-formed in North Queensland in the 1950s with its headquarters in Townsville as North Queensland Squadron, Air Training Corps. No.4 Flight was formed on August 4, 1951 under Flight Lieutenant Harold Honeywell. About 40 cadets joined the unit that paraded at Cairns Central School, later at the Migrant Centre, then at the old Army Drill Hall in Lake St until its move to its present location at the airport. This exact date is not known but it was before 1957.

Many of those early cadets of the 1950s have given our community great stability and they include Stan Carswell, Bob Manning, A. Undy, Lionel Van Dorssen, Bill Cape,

John Crowley, Bob Cleland, R. Bolton, R. Moon and Reg De Boom. Two of the longest serving members of the unit were Alan and Bob Birkbeck, Alan joining in 1955 and Bob in 1957. They both continued after their cadet service ended and became instructors.

Cairns in November 1956 welcomed television, the facility that changed our lives forever, when the ABC began transmitting, with the local commercial station following the next year. Only a few houses in every street had a set and it was a rare privilege to be invited to watch. Many families did what the Hudsons did and packed the kids up soon after an early evening meal, and installed themselves with dozens of others outside the electrical goods shops in Lake St where a few sets were operating. People sat on picnic chairs, cushions, or just stood around to take in the new phenomenon from the windows of Sydney H. Turner

Chairman of the Cairns Harbour Board Cr Cecil Holdcroft, of Herberton, welcomes Italian migrants to the city as they arrive on the SS Flaminia on May 26, 1955.

Picture: Cairns Historical Society

Owen Berzinski of Mossman was one of dozens of runners taking the Olympic Torch through Cairns streets in November 1956 for the Melbourne Games.

at 80 Lake St, and over the road at the sets running in shop windows of Chandlers and Frank Moody, who died Cairns in August 2007 aged 104.

These proprietors used to control the sets in their window by a time switch, but would only run them on nights when they thought they could receive a reasonable picture. It was some years before a transmitter was installed at Bellenden Ker, near Babinda, and the signal for local viewing came from Townsville. Receptions was so poor for most of the time, but people still stayed glued to their sets for an occasional clear sight of faces.

The introduction of television coincided with the Olympic Games in Melbourne and, in the lead up to the big event, Cairns and other Far Northern coastal towns participated in

the Olympic torch relay for the first time. I well remember what a great event that was when Con Verevis – younger brother of Les, a great friend and former schoolmate – led the runners out of Cairns with another great mate, Gordon Perry. On the first leg from the airport to the city, Con Verevis handed the torch to Anthony Mark, an Aboriginal from the Mitchell River community, then it went on to Dennis Nash (Mossman) and Ken Jensen (Cooktown) where the relay halted momentarily for a reception at the council chambers in Abbott St, now occupied by the city library.

Owen Berzinski (Mossman) led the relay from the council chambers on the next leg towards Gordonvale. Most of those 1956 relay runners look back on the event as one of the proudest moments of their lives.

MOMENTS IN TIME

1950 – January 20
ABC radio begins broadcasts in Cairns.

1950 – July 28
Keith Budden, 20, dies after being bitten by a taipan he captured at Edge Hill to milk for the first venom used by the Commonwealth Serum Laboratory to develop an anti-venene.

1951 – June 30
Cominos Cafe closes Abbott St premises after operating there since 1906.

1951 – September 16
Calvary Hospital opens for the Catholic Little Company of Mary at 197-199 Abbott St.

1951 – June 23
First commercial flight of Bush Pilots Airways, founded by Bob (later Sir Robert) Norman.

1951 – August 4
Air Training Corps No. 4 Flight forms in Cairns.

1951 – October 6
100-float pageant ends week-long celebrations of Back to Cairns 75th anniversary observance.

1953 – June 6
First Sunlander train arrives from Brisbane.

1953 – August 4
Demolition of giant fig tree in Abbott St.

1953 – November 6
First public naturalisation ceremony in Cairns when Mrs Itala Imerito took oath of allegiance at annual CWA general meeting.

1954 – March 13
Huge crowds greet Queen Elizabeth on her first visit to Cairns.

1954 – June 26
Underwater observatory opens at Green Island.

1954 – October 7
Intake from Behana Creek almost doubles city's available water supply to more than 20 million litres a day.

1954 – November 24
Cairns and District Tourism Association is formed.

1954 – December 13
Opening night Cairns Little Theatre's first production of J.B. Priestley's *I've Been There* in Central Methodist Hall, Aplin St.

1955 – May 27
SS Flaminia brings first shipload of 550 assisted European migrants to work on sugar cane farms.

1955 – August 5
Cairns Australian National Football League forms at Sea Scouts hall on Esplanade.

1955 – August 6
New two-storey £430,000 ($13 million in

2007) railway station in McLeod St opens.

1956 – March 6
Cyclone Agnes hits Cairns district.

1956 – November 9
Olympic Torch for the Melbourne Games arrives in Cairns from Darwin.

1956 – July 23
First sighting of Michael Fomenko ("Tarzan") paddling canoe in Trinity Inlet.

1956 – September 21
Norman Park renamed Munro Martin Park dedicated to half-sisters Janet Munro and Margaret Hart Martin for their philanthropy.

1956 – October 18
Rockman's in Lake/Shields streets is first Cairns building to be airconditioned.

1957 – November 7
New bridge opens over Freshwater Creek.

1957 – December 18
Premier Nicklin decides against continuing Great Northern Cannery at Smith's Creek after years of financial and supply problems.

1958 – March 20
Sewerage work for city begins with construction of the treatment plant at East Stratford.

1959 – September 10
First race meeting of Cairns Amateurs held at Cannon Park.

DR HUGO FLECKER

H ugo Flecker, a radiologist and naturalist, was one of the most interesting people I have met in my lifetime in Cairns. Flecker wrote a weekly *Nature Topics* article in *The Cairns Post* and it was published continuously between 1935 up to his death in 1957, totalling more than 1000 columns. In this way, he tried to raise public awareness of environmental issues that still concern us today: uncontrolled fires on the city's hillslopes, the threat by introduction of exotic animals like the cane toad, impact of large numbers of tourists visiting potentially fragile areas such as Green Island and Michaelmas Cay, detrimental consequences of soil erosion, and spread of weeds such as lantana.

I was introduced to Flecker when I was a teenager in the late 1940s. A radiologist by profession, he was of average build, usually dressed in a white tropical suit when on duty at his rooms at 52 Abbott St. He had smiling eyes and a gentle manner that belied the tremendous energy he devoted to researching plants and animals of the Cairns region in his spare time. Flecker, who founded the North Queensland Naturalists Club in August 1932 soon after he came to Cairns, ensured his place in history by positively identifying the deadly box jellyfish (named Chironex fleckerii after him) when a boy was stung by one at Cardwell in 1955. Swimmers today are well aware of the menace of the lethal box jellyfish and the smaller Irukandji. But people more than 100 years ago were obviously conscious of the presence of these menaces to bathers as the local newspaper of December 2, 1892 reported that a small boy almost succumbed to the sting of a poisonous (box) jellyfish.

Flecker did much more for this community through his great love of natural history. The NQ Naturalists Club was one of the most active community organisations in this city's history during the 1930s-50s. They held regular field trips

Dr Hugo Flecker, the eminent naturalist and Cairns radiologist who identified the deadly box jellyfish in 1955.

and excursions throughout the region, identifying plants and animals, and met every month when lectures were usually a feature. Many of Cairns's leading business and professional people were members. They included George Brooks, who was my dentist as a child when he had rooms in Lake St; Joe Wyer, long-serving secretary of the Cairns Harbour Board; Ernie Stephens, founder of the Cairns Historical Society who worked for the DPI's research station at Kamerunga; city engineer Frank Morris; Dr Charles Knott; Harry Barkus, a typewriter sales and service business proprietor in Abbott St; and Vince Vlasoff, who built the underwater observatory at Green Island with Lloyd Grigg in 1954.

The Cairns Historical Society has a copy of Flecker's itinerary between 1939 and 1954 which provides the footsteps in his research in identifying the several thousands of plant specimens he collected. He spent years lobbying for a museum to house the specimens. They were once located in a small weatherboard building at the council's Edge Hill gardens and later at Kuranda Barracks, the wartime headquarters for HMAS Cairns, one of several buildings on a reclaimed area of the Esplanade.

Flecker usually spent Saturday between 1-5pm with his collection at Edge Hill and neighbourhood kids often turned up for a free lecture on the taxidermy specimens of NQ fauna, trays and cases of insects, and snakes in alcohol-filled jars that were stored there. Flecker's plant specimens were eventually incorporated in the general collection at the CSIRO at Atherton. A zoo also existed in the Edge Hill

gardens between 1936-50 housing native animals such as cassowaries, wallabies, crocodiles, birds, sugar gliders and wombats. Dr Flecker preferred animals on display in natural settings and would have liked to have seen the zoo developed along the lines of the Healesville Sanctuary in Victoria.

Following a medical congress in Cairns in 1935, Flecker maintained a register of injuries caused by plants and animals, with case histories of incidents and associated research. These included bites from taipans, sudden blindness caused by eating the fruit of the native plant, the finger cherry, and other poisonous creatures including scorpions, stonefish, caterpillars and plants. Unfortunately, the register disappeared around the time of his death and has never been rediscovered.

Flecker died in Calvary Hospital on June 25, 1957 after a short illness. The Cairns City Council in 1971 named the city's gardens at Edge Hill the Flecker Botanic Gardens, some 36 years after Flecker had first inspected them with Mayor Billy Collins and curator Les Wright to convert them to that purpose.

"It is always well to consider the possible evil effects of introduced plants and animals"

– Hugo Flecker, reflecting in his *Nature Notes* column in *The Cairns Post* in May 1935 when the bufo marinus (cane toad) experiment was starting at Gordonvale. The cane toad (right) has become a significant pest in Queensland, posing a threat to many native species and spreading beyond state borders.

Sixteen teams from throughout the district parade down Lake St for a marching girls carnival in Cairns when the movement was at the peak of its popularity in the 1950-60s. The Northernaires (Cairns Municipal Band), Regimentals (Cairns 51st Battalion Band), Bandettes (Cairns Combined Schools Band), Fitzgeralds Innisfail (Innisfail Citizens Band) and Cairns Midgets were among those taking part.

CHAPTER FOUR - 1960s

The first major change to the city's landscape of my childhood took place when the Cairns City Council embarked upon a huge reclamation scheme in the early 1960s. The project involved filling in Alligator Creek, a substantial watercourse with headwaters behind the Cairns Showground. This creek once drained the city's central swamp area and flowed through what is now Barlow Park, across Spence St under rail and road bridges about 50m west of the Severin St intersection, meandering around the Cairns Timber Ltd (site of today's council chambers), then running almost directly south in a line with Draper St to empty into Trinity Inlet at Smith's Creek.

Fishermen moored their boats at a jetty where Hartley and Draper streets now intersect, and at other locations along the creek's banks. I spent hundreds of my leisure hours on and around Alligator Creek with my great childhood mate, the late Ron Beecheno. We often swam there and one of our delights was to ride fast ebbing high tides from the Hartley St jetty to the mouth. I shudder to think of the times that crocodiles, which I have since learned were captured there at times, might have contemplated us as their supper. I have seen a photo in Cairns Historical Society records of a sizeable croc being caught there in the 1930s by one of the Schridde brothers, who ran a zoo at Browns Bay, a former popular resort near Second Beach.

In its wake, the reclamation scheme caused the demolition of a colourful shanty town settlement known as Malaytown, a collection of huts on Alligator Creek near its mouth as it joined Smith's Creek. Malaytown was established in the 1890s by fishermen who chose the creek for its safe and convenient moorings. They built houses on its banks and tied their boats alongside rickety wooden jetties. It was given its name because most early inhabitants were of Malayan descent. They came to work on sugar plantations being

Old Malaytown, a residential part of Cairns near Smith's Creek, disbanded early 1960s during extensive reclamation of the area, including Alligator Creek which once flowed through the land now occupied by the council chambers.

established in the Cairns district in the 1880s.

The settlement made headlines in the *Morning Post* of March 15, 1904 when a resident died during an outbreak of bubonic plague. Health Department inspectors moved in and 16 humpies were burnt to the ground to contain the outbreak. The paper described Malaytown as "a motley township inhabited by Chinese, Japanese, Javanese, Malays and Cingalese". New huts were soon built and occupied. The population became large enough for a police station to be established there from 1909 until 1934. The settlement steadily evolved into a multicultural community with Hindus, Aborigines, Torres Strait and South Sea Islanders, and Filipinos moving in to take up residence with people from other countries already there.

I spent most of my childhood living in Hartley St and Bunda St, only a few hundred metres away. I often passed through Malaytown when Ron Beecheno and I rowed our old flattie down the creek to drop our crab pots and fishing lines around the main wharves. Most of the friendly inhabitants were skilled fishermen. They built their own flat-bottomed boats and made their nets. They fished in the inlet and caught prawns around the mouth of the Barron River. Many of their children attended Central State School in Lake St, where the Oasis Resort was later built. Others were pupils at Parramatta during my time there from 1936-44. Many of their makeshift huts were made from mangrove timber and other scrap items. The settlement had no electricity and town water was not connected until the 1940s.

Malaytown was, in essence, an early example of multiculturalism working successfully. People from the regular community interacted with its residents through a mutual interest in fishing and music. Among the best-known families were the Pitts. Patriarch was Douglas Pitt junior, a Torres Strait Islander whose father was born in Jamaica. Doug Pitt, who moved to Cairns from the Torres Strait in 1905, was renowned for his marathon swimming exploits. He

Lake St in the early 1960s on installation of sewerage in Cairns, estimated to cost about $40 million in today's dollars. Work started in March 1958 to build the treatment plant at East Stratford. Expected to be completed in March 1963, work covered the area from the Esplanade to Severin St, the wharves to Cairns North, and included some of the residential parts of Edge Hill.

Picture: Cairns Historical Society

Staff of Penneys in Abbott St in the mid-1950s. Penneys employed some 70-80 staff at its Abbott St store until taken over by G.J. Coles in 1956. Coles closed three Penneys branches in Shields, Bunda and Sheridan streets and expanded the Abbott St store, which it boasted as being the city's first supermarket.

swam in rough seas to shore in Cairns after his fishing boat was swamped during a cyclone near Green Island in March 1918. He was the first man to swim from Magnetic Island to Townsville in November 1921. His children, Heather, Dulcie, Sophie, Wally and Len, were all gifted musicians. Dulcie, who assumed the stage name of Georgia Lee after World War II, became an international star as did their niece, Wilma Reading. The Pitts moved out of Malaytown in the late 1920s. I remember them living in Spence St, Bungalow, a few doors east of Buchan St. Len Pitt and his wife Esme were once my neighbours. We have enjoyed a friendship over many years, beginning in our teenage days in rugby league.

Others who lived in Malaytown during my childhood included the Jacobs, Ware, Guivarra, Watkin, Sailor, Binsiar and Savage families. Many former residents look back on their lives at Malaytown with great affection in what was a caring and happy community. Herb Sang, a respected Cairns businessman who was the city's biggest wholesale and retail fruit and vegetable merchant for many years, lived there as a child until about 1930. His father George rented a house in Kenny St where he ran a mixed business soon after they moved to Cairns from Babinda. "I remember it as a happy time of my life," Herb told me some years ago. "The people we dealt with from Malaytown were pleasant and always neatly dressed and well behaved."

Cairns branches of major wholesale merchants, Cummins & Campbell Ltd, Samuel Allen & Sons and Burns Philp, once dominated the commercial sector of Cairns, providing secure employment for more than 400 people and many more in branches throughout North Queensland. These merchants were the middle men between manufacturers and retailers, including the region's dozens of small corner stores. They also supplied goods in bulk to large cattle stations on Cape York Peninsula and the Gulf. They traded in every commodity imaginable from hardware, paint and building materials, groceries, confectionery, stationery, produce, horse and poultry feed, and beer, ales, wines and spirits. Support for the merchants began to wane in the 1960s when grocery supermarkets, so commonplace over the past few decades, started to make their mark after G.J. Coles took over the Penneys chain of stores in Cairns in April 1956. They expanded the main store at 83-87 Abbott St, publicising its development as being the city's first supermarket. It also closed three outer grocery store branches in Shields, Bunda and Sheridan streets, but continued trading as Penneys until it began using the Coles name in 1964.

Many Cairns people up to the 1960s did not travel into the CBD often, even from what are now the city's inner suburbs. They shopped almost exclusively at their corner grocery store and butcher, had milk and bread delivered daily, and fruit and vegetables brought to their door once a week, invariably by an old Chinese market gardener, carrying his produce in two baskets balanced at the ends of a pole over his shoulder or pushing a two-wheel cart.

Men working for the Rawleigh and Watkins companies, manufacturers of patent medicines, essences, toilet preparations and other household products, were other regular house-to-house callers, hawking products like Rawleigh's Antiseptic Salve ("for man and beast", according to the label), Watkins Menthol Camphor Ointment and Watkins Petro-Carbo Salve. The J.R. Watkins company advertised opportunities for salesmen in the late 1940s stating they could earn each week from £8-12 (up to $720 today).

Households ran up weekly accounts with their corner shopkeepers and settled in cash on pay day on Friday. They included the Lazarus brothers and Taffy George (Bungalow), George Mooney (Lyons St), Les Beh (Earlville), Penridges and Bradfords (Edge Hill), Skarotts (Stratford), Gallo & Cattana (Redlynch), Colin Penridge (Edge Hill), the Tibaldi brothers and Mrs Ludlow (Martyn St), Lee Moon (opposite today's Cape York Hotel), Jack Coulthard (Fiveways) and

the Kellers (Sheridan St). A visit to the CBD travelling by bus was more of a social day out although people might buy a few specials at the larger CBD grocery outlets.

Cairns had five major grocery stores in the CBD vying for a share of the household budget with busy corner shops in every suburb. All five city stores ran display advertisements with "specials" in *The Cairns Post* every week in the 1940-50s in a competitive market, offering free delivery. Those in the city had plenty to choose from with Brightways and Armstrong, Ledlie & Stillman (AL&S) on the western side of Lake St and Manahans and Bolands on the opposite side of the street where men in long white aprons behind wooden counters, gnarled and polished to a smooth finish by years of wear, provided us with real service.

Bolands, near the Spence St corner in Lake St, was considered the major retail outlet of Cairns until 1963 when they sold to David Jones. Eric Lund, Joe Donnelly, Bobby Williamson, Arthur Maunder, Jim Shambrook and Gus Brady worked in the grocery department. As a child, I loved going there with my mother. I still have a sense of how the rich array of foodstuffs stored in bulk, the sides of bacon, legs of hams, blocks of cheese, assorted spices, tubs of sugar, rice and flour, biscuits, dried fruits and dozens of other items, produced such a delicious aroma.

Brightways had their store in Lake St near Westpac today. Two Chinese brothers, William (known as "Narm") and Harry Young, owned it. Fred, a younger brother and partner, died in the 1930s. The Youngs were entrepreneurial for their time, and delivered orders to customers as far south as Babinda. H.A. Manahan & Sons, a Brisbane-based chain with stores throughout Queensland, were across the road, next to the pharmacy operated by Charles Herries.

Les Horn was manager in the mid-1930s, and Arthur Keller, Con Lazarus, Bill Ireland, Norma Roberts, Arthur Nicholls and Frank Allen-Aitkens were others who worked at Manahans at various times.

AL&S had a wider range of goods as well as a grocery section. AL&S began in 1899 at Herberton, founded by

Staff at Armstrong Ledlie & Stillman's store in Lake St, next to Hides Hotel, circa 1930s. AL&S was one of four major grocery stores in Lake St. The others were Bolands, Brightways and Manahans. They all closed in the face of competition from modern supermarkets when Woolworths and Coles came to Cairns. AL&S closed in 1974.

H.J. (Herbert) Armstrong, John Ledlie and W.E. (William) Stillman. When the Cairns store opened on November 1, 1910, it advertised as "general merchants, grocers, provision dealers" and importers of general merchandise, hardware, glassware, chinaware, crockeryware and (this item has me stumped) "oilmen's stores".

AL&S staff in the 1930s included George Davison (accountant), Harry Harpin and Eric Gordon (men's wear), Miss King and Myrtle Lavern (millinery, haberdashery, drapery). Albert Henry (Jack) Dean was a familiar figure in Cairns in the 1920-30s as AL&S's orderman. He rode a horse around Cairns households to collect orders which were

made up and delivered that afternoon by Bill Petith and Bill Robertson by horse and cart. AL&S closed its Cairns store in 1974 and southern-based retailer Waltons took over.

The face of grocery retailing in the Cairns region began changing in the early 1960s when both Manahans and Brightways closed in the face of intense competition from a new Woolworths BCC Food Fair in Abbott St and a branch at Edge Hill, and the expanded Coles-Penneys outlet in Abbott St. The entry into Cairns of grocery chains and supermarkets from the 1960s brought about a change in the way of trading and signalled the demise of wholesale merchants that supplied goods to the small corner shops. They had been among the

Burns Philp, pictured with staff outside the Abbott St building in the 1930s, was one of several wholesale merchants in Cairns until supermarkets changed the face of retailing from the early 1970s. It ceased trading in 1978 and the building was demolished in October 1983 after it was deemed to have been unsafe. The Cairns International Hotel, 17 Abbott St, now occupies much of the former Burns Philp site.

city's biggest employers for more half a century.

Competition from the bigger chains forced the suburban shops to try to compete. They had to become more price-competitive if they were to survive, and formed groups to buy direct from manufacturers instead of through local merchants. Lou Piccone, who today owns the IGA supermarkets at Edmonton and Brinsmead, was a driving force from his Edmonton store behind a group that began trading in 1962 under the name of "K" (standing for "king" quality) stores. They later became the Family Fare group with at least 25

members in the Cairns area and more in the region. Other retailers joined a smaller Cairns-based group operating under the Foodland name. Wholesale merchants suffered in turn.

Cummins & Campbell's branch had traded in Cairns from 1906. The building it occupied still stands on the corner of Grafton and Spence streets. It was built in the 1920s with a second storey added in 1930. It had other warehouses further south in Grafton St and on the corner of Dutton and Spence streets. Its managers in the 1940-60s included Jack Birch, Stan McKeown, Jack MacCallum and George Stevens.

Samuel Allen was in Lake St where the Playpen nightclub used to be. David Olley, H.M. Podosky, Bert Jones and Arthur Drew were some of its managers. The firm established a warehouse on that site in 1916 and added office space in 1925. C&C's and Allen's were North Queensland companies with head offices in Townsville.

Burns Philp was by far the biggest with head office in Sydney, outlets throughout Papua New Guinea and the South Pacific, and branches at Thursday Island, Cooktown, Normanton and Innisfail. It established a presence in Cairns soon after settlement. In 1900, it occupied a large building with offices and warehouse where the Cairns International Hotel is now at 17 Abbott St. The two-storey building ran through the block with a rear entrance on Lake St. Daniel Patience, mayor of Cairns in 1893-94, was an early manager.

Others in later years included Percy Swan, Bill Dupain, Vivian Noble, Charlie Taylor, Bob Stone and Tom Wood. Dupain was a long-serving manager around the World War II years. He lived in Abbott St where Matson Plaza is now in an old plantation-style Queenslander. It was set well back in a large allotment with tall palms growing on a neat lawn in the front. My grandfather, Fred Hudson, lived there as resident gardener/caretaker. I visited him there as a lad in the 1930s.

These merchants had huge fleets of trucks that seemed to be constantly on the move picking up goods from ship and rail. They then delivered to various depots large consignments of orders packed in wooden cases and cartons to be sent by road, rail or sea through transport firms to customers in far-flung parts of Far North Queensland. They also acted as agents for the Cairns Brewery, manufacturer of the once-famous Cairns Draught bulk beer. Although the brewery delivered bulk beer direct to hotels or consigned it by rail and road to outlets throughout North Queensland, hotels ordered and paid for it through wholesale merchants.

Thomas Brown & Sons was another merchant that traded for a short period in the 1950-60s from premises fronting Sheridan St where Coles had a store in recent years. Jue Sue Agencies was another smaller merchant. Two smaller firms,

Joseph Pease (Abbott St) and P.J. Doyle (Lake St), traded exclusively in beer, ales, wines and spirits.

Headricks was a locally-owned and operated merchandising firm employing a staff of about 65 at one time. Dave Headrick started it in 1905 in Lake St a few doors south of Hides Hotel. He operated the business with his son Bill and then with Bill's son David from Spence St premises.

In the early days, they sold farm-related goods and produce, but with the introduction of mechanisation from the 1950s they specialised in agricultural machinery parts and engineering supplies, steel and wire products, roofing materials, as well as produce and other goods. The firm sold out to Burns Philp in 1972 and closed in 1975.

The merchants employed teams of sales representatives selling their wares to grocery stores, hotels and other retailers throughout Far North Queensland. These commercial travellers, once referred to by a historian as "the knights of the road", were often better known than the firms they represented. The first commercial traveller I knew was Henry Johns, who worked for Burns Philp when I was a child.

He lived near my grandmother Marion Hudson whose tiny two-room cottage was on the corner of Severin and Grove streets. Among other travellers I knew in the 1950-60s were Alex Campbell, for many years Cairns Cricket Association chairman; Bob Stone, Charlie Armstrong, Fred Tolcher, Andy Hansen, Bert Stanley, Bob Cowie (Burns Philp), Len McKillop, Frank Gay, Fred Mellick, Mick Carroll, Terry Fowler and Cec Tyson (Cummins & Campbell). Others were Jim Palmer, Brian Chamberlain, Jim Cowan, Max Martin, Reg Dean, Lowell Amies, Jack Walters (Samuel Allen), Ron Ireland (Joseph Pease), Les Pedersen, Ron Petrie (P.J. Doyle), Tom Ireland, Waley Jones, Geoff Lucas (Thomas Brown), and Allan Amos (Jue Sue Agencies). I worked at Cummins & Campbell in the 1950s as a trainee salesman, taking over their routes when Len ("Curley") McKillop, a former champion cricketer and footballer and their coastal representative, and Cec Tyson, based at Atherton, took annual leave.

Hotels where the sales reps stayed provided sample rooms

The Cairns brewery, corner Spence and Draper streets, once provided employment for a few hundred locals. It was established in 1925 and ceased brewing operations in February 1992.

for travellers to display their goods, often in separate small buildings at the rear of their main premises. Some reps worked late into the evening hosting their clients. The sample room concept was introduced at the Queensland Commercial Travellers Association's behest in 1916. The QCTA later rated hotels according to the facilities and concessions they provided for its members.

The QCTA was formed in January 1884. By 1927, it had 1492 registered members and this number steadily increased until World War II. The QCTA acquired its own building in Brisbane. It had a liquor licence and served meals for members and their guests. It provided similar facilities for many years in Flinders St, Townsville.

As a sign of the times, the QCTA had only 16 registered members at its annual general meeting in 1995. Modern technology and new ways of doing business left former "knights of the road" with only happy memories of a camaraderie and fellowship they once enjoyed.

Two other major employers in the city then were Cairns Timber Ltd and the Cairns Brewery, located in Spence St at opposite sides of Draper St. A friend once described the scene at this intersection at knock-off time on weekdays as resembling the start of the Tour de France with a horde of workers setting off on their bicycles for home or to their nearest pub.

A group of businessmen formed the Cairns Brewing Co. Ltd in June 1924. With J.L. Breheny as chairman and head brewer, the company tapped its first batch of ale on July 7, 1925. But locals did not fancy the new brew and, hindered by a lack of finance and technical skills, the company was forced into liquidation. It re-formed on September 3, 1927 as Northern Australian Breweries Ltd with new finance. David Headrick, a local businessman, took over briefly as chairman of directors, and Captain Charles de Bavay was managing director and head brewer. However, Northern Australian Breweries did not make much progress until Reg

Fogarty took over as managing director in 1930. Because of limited production, Cairns Draught was sold only as far south as Cardwell with most sales in Cairns and Innisfail. Main opposition to the local brew was from Carlton beer and, at one stage, merchants handling the southern product tried to make inroads into Cairns Draught sales in Innisfail by reducing the price of a pot from sixpence to threepence.

But the Innisfail drinkers remained fiercely loyal to the local brew, although Reg Fogarty went to Melbourne to try to convince the Carlton bosses that it was in both their interests to end the price war. It turned out they knew nothing about it, but gave instructions that the price-cutting should stop. Fogarty's visit stirred Carlton's interest in the Cairns operation and on September 21, 1941, NAB directors decided to accept Melbourne's takeover offer. The NAB name continued until 1972 when the company operated as Carlton & United Breweries (NQ) Ltd, to be changed again

in July 1986 to Carlton & United Breweries (Queensland) Ltd. Fogarty went on to become general manager of Carlton in Melbourne and managers who followed him at Cairns included Coogie Kelly, Morrie Horton, Peter Forness and Chris Johnson.

Cairns Draught was so popular that hotels also sold it in 26-ounce (two litre) bottles that they filled themselves. Some working men's hotels, such as the National (now Cape York) and Queens, sold about half of their total output in their own bottled beer. Beer was delivered to local hotels every day and regularly by rail and road transport to hotels throughout North Queensland. Truck drivers were as well known as senior staff. They included Cec Wilson, Arthur Nash and his son Geoff, Gundy Brown, Les Baker, Harold (Oozie) Barton, a Cairns representative rugby league full-back, and Pat Keeley.

The brewery produced other packaged beer in NQ Lager, Cairns Bitter Ale and Gold Top Pale Ale. Cairns drinkers,

Cairns Timber Ltd, on the Spence St site of today's council chambers, was one of several sawmills in the city and one of Cairns's biggest employers.

loyal to the local brews for many years, began switching to national brands in the 1970s-80s. The company, after so long as one of the region's model workplaces with a total staff of up to 350, went through an unhappy time late in the 1980s when many workers lost their jobs through redundancies. It eventually became uneconomical to produce local products here and brewing operations ceased in February 1992.

Cairns Timber Ltd likewise provided job security for many men, seemingly for life, and it was inconceivable to Cairns people in early postwar years that it would ever close its doors. Many long-established Cairns families will recall they had at least one of their men employed at the CTL and, it seemed to me as a lad, that every second household in their vicinity depended on the mill or the brewery for their livelihood. My brother Bill worked at the mill after he left school aged 14, as did many of his mates.

CTL operated from the property now occupied by the council chambers, bounded by Draper and Spence streets, with Alligator Creek, reclaimed early in the 1960s, snaking along the southern and western borders of the main part of the mill. At the peak of its operations, CTL employed nearly 500 people in various branches and it was a blow to the city's economy when the Cairns mill closed in May 1966 after it was sold to the Brisbane-based Hancock Brothers.

CTL was formed in 1909 with 20 employees. It took over two established sawmills in Spence St. Thomas Griffiths, regarded by many as the pioneer of sawmilling in Cairns, operated one from May 1899. R.A. Tills, who previously owned a mill at Redlynch in partnership with Louis Severin, had moved to Spence St in 1898. George Michael Gummow was the first general manager until his death in 1926 when his son, George Douglas Gummow, took over and remained in that position until he died in 1958.

CTL expanded under GD's management. He visited the United States in 1931 and, as a result of that trip, established the veneer industry in North Queensland by setting up a complete veneer mill in Cairns. Experts from the US helped to set it up and train local workers. CTL branched into other installations at Yungaburra, Kuranda and Innisfail and once had a private tramline with hardwood rails of about 6.5km in length in the Ravenshoe district to haul timber to Turelca siding on the main railway between Tumoulin and Kaban. Sawn timber, veneer and plywood from CTL's various plants found markets Australia-wide and in the UK, US, Far East, New Zealand and South Africa. The floor of London's House of Commons, destroyed by bombing in World War II, was replaced with Queensland walnut, much of it from Cairns. The Speaker's chair was made from North Queensland black bean and Queensland walnut was used in the Houses of Parliament in Northern Ireland.

CTL once had its own vessel, Wortanna that carried timber between Cairns, Townsville and Brisbane. It was sold to the Adelaide Steamship Company which used it as a sugar lighter. Previously, CTL owned a schooner named Tom Fisher that sailed between Thursday Island, Cairns and Townsville. CTL diversified. It formed the Cairns Cottage Company in the 1920s. It subdivided land opposite the mill and sold most of the properties to mill workers. It formed another successful subsidiary, CTL Glass and Hardware, operating over the road from the mill in Spence St.

One aspect of CTL's operations not generally known is its links with the successful Kangaroos Football Club through a club named Woodpeckers that fielded teams in both rugby league and cricket competitions in Cairns during World War II. Woodpeckers teams were made up mainly of men who worked at CTL and their friends. John Dunstan, a mill employee and one of the most influential figures in both sports in Cairns for many years, was the driving force behind the club and a prominent member of both the senior footy and cricket teams. Members of the Woodpeckers senior and junior footy sides, including John Dunstan, George McFarlane, Norrie Barr, Keith Mendo, Hec Lesina, Keith Johns and Gordon Farrelly, were associated later with Kangaroos when they resumed in the Cairns competition in 1946. I was one of many youngsters who spent much of their leisure time playing in and around the mill and on many of its sawdust

Loading bagged sugar provided the bulk of work for up to 1000 waterside workers employed on Cairns wharves before bulk loading of sugar was introduced in October 1964 and the containerisation of other cargoes around the same time.

heaps. I recall as a lad joining Woodpeckers cricketers at practice after work on a half-length concrete pitch near one of the mill's sheds in Draper St when it was a cul-de-sac, running only a couple of hundred metres past Spence St.

Up to 1000 men were once employed on Cairns wharves to handle huge cargoes from coastal steamers that were the only links with southern cities before the railway from Brisbane was completed on December 10, 1924. The bulk of export cargoes were timber and bagged sugar manufactured in several of the district's sugar mills. The raw sugar was packed in 160-pound (73kg) hessian bags and stored in sheds on mill grounds ready for transport by rail to the nearest major port of Townsville or Cairns. The bags were loaded directly into railway wagons if they were available, but most of the time they were stored in the huge sheds on the main wharves until the larger ships arrived to take them away.

Much of the bagged sugar, particularly from the Mossman Mill, was transported to Cairns by sea on lighters. Port Douglas had a sizeable waterside workforce during the season, which often lasted from May to December. Regular lighters operating in the Cairns district from Port Douglas and Mourilyan harbour were the Herbert, Carroo, Goondi, Katoora, Toorie, Karalta, Korara and Konanda. The lighters were under the control of the Adelaide Steamship Company which had staff at Port Douglas, Mourilyan Harbour and Cairns to supervise their operations. The days of the sugar lighters and bagged sugar came to an end when bulk loading was introduced, first with the opening of the terminal at Mourilyan in October 1960, and the other at Cairns in October 1964. The last shipment of bagged sugar left Cairns wharves for Korea on June 30, 1964 on the Rae Maersk.

Nowhere has the development of the CBD area of Cairns had a greater impact than on our hotels where 60 years ago a resident population barely one-tenth of today's supported 22 pubs in the main city area. With some hotels transferring their licences as the suburbs grew in the late 1960s, only seven of those 22 hotels are still operating on the same site with their premises retained in much the same way as they were half a century ago. The famous Barbary Coast, stretching a few hundred metres from the corner of Lake and Wharf streets down the first block of Abbott St, had six hotels, the Royal, Oceanic, Empire (now Barrier Reef), Mining Exchange, Australian and Criterion, operating cheek-by-jowl and catering to the huge waterside workforce and workers in the area employed by wholesale merchants and government departments. Only the Barrier Reef has survived.

The Pacific and Strand, two of the city's better class hotels on the Esplanade, were demolished to make way for today's Pacific International, the Strand closing late in 1962 and the Pacific about 20 years later. Other city hotels that have disappeared include the Post Office (later Great Northern), opposite *The Cairns Post*; the Court House, first occupied in 1884 about where Woolworths' loading bay is in Abbott St today; the Imperial, corner of Abbott and Shields streets; and the Palace in Lake St, which was demolished to make way for the relocation of the Commonwealth Bank from Abbott St in 1973. The Central Hotel, built in 1908-09, no longer operates as a hotel but fortunately this lovely old building has been retained in much the same way. The Federal and Newmarket, on diagonally opposite corners of the intersection of Grafton and Spence streets, have long since been demolished as has

the Queens on the corner of Aplin and McLeod streets. Some of the old city licences were transferred to the new hotels that began popping up in the suburbs in the 1970s, including the Bungalow in Aumuller St, Newmarket (Pease St) and Balaclava (Mulgrave Rd).

A few of the old city hotels depended for much of their income on out-of-town visitors and the southern tourist trade that arrived mainly by coastal steamer and rail, but most were supported by locals. These pubs drew on a vast array of shop assistants, clerks and blue-collar workers for their trade, and they included employees of banks, government offices, the wholesale merchants Cummins & Campbell, Burns Philp and Samuel Allen & Co, the railway, Cairns Brewery and Cairns Timber Limited, and a workforce of up to 1000 thirsty wharfies in the days before the introduction of bulk-loading of sugar and container cargoes during the 1960s.

There were no suburban hotels or sporting clubs like Brothers or Cazalys, and not a licensed outlet west of the National (now Cape York) until Woree, or north of the city after the Queens Hotel (corner Aplin and McLeod) until Stratford. The only two licensed lawn bowls clubs were in the main city area, with the Cairns club in Lake St opposite St John's Anglican Church, and the Masonic club in Abbott St, a few doors south of today's city library.

City pubs did a brisk trade weekdays between 5-6.30 pm in

Three hotels along Wharf St, the Royal, Oceanic and Empire (later Barrier Reef), did a thriving trade when the Cairns wharves had a workforce of about 1000 men up to the time bulk sugar loading began in the 1960s.

Most musical, social and theatrical events in Cairns were once held at the Hibernian Hall, corner Lake and Florence streets, from 1906 when it was built until it closed in October 1968. It was demolished the next year. Hundreds of service personnel spent many hours of their leave there during World War II when the Catholic United Services Auxiliary took over the upstairs section used as the Irish Association's clubrooms. More than 160,000 troops attended in 1942 alone.

the days before drink-driving became a major traffic problem. Regardless, few average workers drove a motor vehicle. They would knock over their six to eight beers, then catch a bus or pedal their bike to their home in the suburbs. Many of the city hotels enjoyed patronage from sporting clubs which used the pubs for their committee meetings and after-match celebrations, and players and supporters usually congregated at those hotels.

Kangaroos footballers always gathered at the Grand Hotel when the licensees in earlier years included Kevin Fransen, Joe Ferguson and Merv McHugh, while Ivanhoes made the Crown (Jack Harvey and Andy Maule) or Mining Exchange (Angelo Papas) their headquarters. Brothers at various times were associated with the Queens (Bill Allendorf), Central ("Wacky" Lang and Tom Kennedy), and the Australian (George Fitzpatrick), and the now-defunct Uniteds usually met at the Empire (Barrier Reef). Cairns lifesavers could always be found at the Imperial in the days of Mal Baumgarten, Frank Atkins and Brad Brandenburg, cricketers and soccer players had their favourite hotels, while the sailing fraternity usually drank at the Australian or Mining Exchange when they were not over at the Aquatic Club.

Fifty years ago, with pubs depending so much on the locals for their living, patrons would expect to see the licensee behind the bar during the midday and late afternoon sessions.

Astute publicans like Bailey Pitt (Federal and Strand), Eileen Pennington (Commercial), Jack Loth (Imperial) and Cec Edwards (Newmarket) would know every customer by name, where they worked, what he usually drank, something of his family history, and would often lend an ear for a tale of woe or access to their wallet for a pound or two to tide them over until payday. That was the sort of personal interaction between publican and customer that was expected.

Most pubs had a "ladies' lounge", which was the only place women were allowed to be served until the laws were changed around this time, and some city hotels had their saloon bars, which afforded a little privacy for businessmen and their clients. Women were never to be served a drink in the public bars although the bar attendants were almost exclusively female, while men were usually employed as drink waiters in the lounge and for dinner dances at some of the better class hotels like the Strand, Pacific and Hides, where I remember Tom Langtree, Fred Biancotti, Ron Kelly and Sid Downs dressed in black trousers, long white shirt and black bow tie. In those days, there was only one beer on tap: Cairns Draught that was brewed in Cairns and distributed throughout North Queensland from the Mackay district in the south, west to Mount Isa, and north to Thursday Island. Cairns Draught was also the most popular packaged beer, bottled on the premises by almost every hotel.

MOMENTS IN TIME

1961 – April 8
Blue Nursing Service is established in Cairns with Sister Baird in charge.

1961 – April 14
Coral Drive-in cinema opens at Woree.

1961 – July
Manoora is last of coastal passenger ships to be withdrawn from service.

1962 – March 24
Tobruk Memorial Pool opens in Sheridan St, North Cairns.

1962 – May 26
Opening of new Green Island jetty and city's first annual festival which became known as Fun in the Sun.

1962 – December 8
All weather radar and cyclone warning station opens at Saddle

Mountain, Kuranda.

1963 – February 26
Strand Hotel, corner Spence St and Esplanade, is demolished.

1963 – March 31
First water flows over Tinaroo Dam.

1963 – September 7
Barron Falls power station officially opened.

1964 – January 30
New Cairns automatic telephone exchange begins operating.

1964 – April 2
Pacific Resort Hotel at Yorkeys Knob is destroyed by fire. It was never rebuilt.

1964 – October 3
Bulk sugar loading terminal opens at Cairns wharves.

1965 – September 6
Parking meters began to operate in Cairns CBD at a charge of one shilling an hour.

1965 – November 26
The Cairns Post is bought by Queensland Press Pty Ltd, publishers of *The Courier-Mail* newspaper.

1965 – November 30
New 7000ft runway opens for use at Cairns airport.

1966 – April 29
Microwave radio link opens between Brisbane and Cairns.

1966 – May 11
Last log sawn as major employer Cairns Timber Ltd closes on Spence St site now occupied by council chambers.

Dozens of girls in the Cairns district lost their jobs when manual telephone exchanges became redundant with the introduction of automatic dialing on January 30, 1964. Girls who worked on the manual exchanges formed a strong bond of friendship and many from as far back as the 1940s still meet regularly today.

MOMENTS IN TIME

1966 – September 25
First 1000-pound marlin caught in waters off Cairns, starting a wave of international attention from big game fishermen.

1966 – July 25
ABC's temporary TV station ABNQ9 opens in Cairns.

1966 – September 7
FNQ Channel 10, Cairns's first commercial TV station, opens.

1966 – October 9
Good Samaritan nursing home opens at corner of Tuills and Gatton streets.

1967 – July 29
Bethlehem Home for the Aged opens in Gatton St.

1968 – March 29
Last regular DC3 flight from Cairns to gulf stations.

1968 – April 8
First passenger Ansett jet air service from Brisbane reaches Cairns (TAA on April 10).

1968 – July 8
St Monica's Cathedral in Abbott St is consecrated.

1968 – August 9
First traffic lights operate at Five Ways, Parramatta Park.

1969 – March
Demolition of Hibernian Hall in Lake St, where most of the city's musical and theatrical performances were once held.

George Bransford (left) and Richard Obach with 1064lb black marlin Orbach caught off Cairns in 1966, the first 1000-pounder caught in local waters.

THEN AND NOW

The changing face of Cairns over the past three quarters of a century is portrayed in these "then and now" images of several well-known city sites.

Youngsters try their hand at fishing at high tide from the Esplanade retaining wall, opposite the old Mulgrave Shire Offices at 51 The Esplanade, circa 1960s. It presents an entirely different picture now with the opening of the Esplanade Lagoon in 2003, a new boardwalk and other public amenities.

Picture: Cairns Historical Society

Cairns railway station, circa 1940s, was built in 1887 when the Cairns-Kuranda rail line was being constructed. It was replaced with a new building in 1955 that was demolished in 1996 to make way for the Cairns Central shopping complex which opened in 1997.

Picture: Cairns Historical Society

The tree-lined Cairns District (later Base) Hospital, circa 1930s, was the city's third public hospital with work starting in 1912. The first was established in 1878 on the corner of Aplin and Shields streets, and the second in 1885 on the present Esplanade site. The present hospital was redeveloped as part of a massive $127 million building program in the late 1990s.

Picture: Cairns Historical Society

Cairns police station – circa 1930s with the Lands Office (left) on the Esplanade near the Shields St intersection – was built in 1911. The wooden structure was replaced with a new police station in the late 1970s. It moved to a new location in Grafton St in November 1992. The new Outrigger Cairns Resort and specialty shops opened on the site in 2001.

Picture: Cairns Historical Society

Samuel Smith, a bricklayer, built this lovely home (left) at 223 Esplanade for his wife Violet and their family in 1934. The Deeb family built holiday units there in 1978, then opened Acacia Court in 1989. The popular Charlie's Restaurant is named in memory of the late Charlie Deeb who died in 1995.

Picture: Cairns Historical Society.

A view of the former city baths with the Strand Hotel in the right background, circa 1930s. They were the first concrete baths in Cairns and opened on May 9, 1931. They closed during construction of the Tobruk Memorial Pool at North Cairns which opened on March 24, 1962. For a few years, the old site operated as an oceanarium. It is now the site of the Cairns Hilton which was built in 1986.

Picture: Cairns Historical Society

Estate H.S. Williams in Shields St, circa 1930s, next to the Crown Hotel, was once one of Cairns's biggest motor dealers. Sir Sydney Williams, one of the founders of the Cairns Amateurs, was its manager. This area is now the site of some of the city's most popular restaurants.

Picture: Cairns Historical Society

Cairns ambulance started in Cairns on the corner of Sheridan and Spence streets in 1904 and transferred to new premises on the corner of Grafton and Aplin streets, with the official opening (pictured right) in 1927. The centre moved to Anderson St in July 1995, but the building has been retained. The Marquis apartments complex next door (above) was completed in 2007.

Racegoers gather around the saddling enclosure at a Cairns Amateurs meeting at Cannon Park in the 1960s.

Chapter five - Sport

Sport has played a big part in my life, as a player, administrator, commentator and reporter, and always as an enthusiastic spectator. My involvement has given me countless hours of enjoyment, brought me into the company of many interesting characters, and helped to form many lasting friendships.

Like most youngsters of my generation, I played my first sport kicking a rolled-up sugar bag around in scratch rugby league games on the grassy railway reserve opposite our rented house in Bunda St, and put bat to ball for the first time in games of rounders with the neighbourhood kids. We had very little organised sport at either Parramatta State School or Cairns High, possibly because of economic downturn in the Great Depression years of the 1930s and wartime restrictions in the early 1940s. There were no organisations dedicated specifically to junior sport in my childhood and development programs for promising youngsters were light years away into the future. Talent for the most part just simmered away until teenagers were able to join a club at the lowest senior level.

My first involvement in competitive sport came when I joined the Cairns Amateur Swimming Club in 1945 at age 14 and swam in races on Friday night at the old City Baths in Wharf St, where the Hilton Cairns is today.

I learned to swim there in the 1930s. The pool was filled with seawater, flushed every day, and emptied and refilled every 48 hours. Top swimmers in my time included Mick Burrows, Mick Barrett and Dot Battle. I remember the officials who ran the meetings were Jack Plunkett, Eddie Pollard, Watty Sykes, Jock Young, Bob Beattie, Tom Farrugia, and Ron and Norma McKauge. Cairns swimming gained nationwide recognition in December 1933 when its five-man team of Norm Wedlock, Mick Barrett, Harvey O'Neill, Roy Sprecher and Bill Fleming set a Queensland record for the 500-yard "flying squadron", a five-man relay race. They later established an Australian record for the event and Fleming went on to win an Australian championship.

I was on the organising committee of a carnival at the City Baths in which the 1956 Olympic Games team took part.

Annual trophy presentation day at Cairns Bowls Club, corner Minnie and Lake streets in 1926. Cairns Bowls Club and Cairns Golf Club were the only licensed premises outside hotels until well after World War II. Many of the city's business and professional men were members and used the club to socialise after work and at weekends.

The biggest crowd for a cricket match at Griffiths Park in Cairns in April 1952 saw a visiting team from Sydney, including Test greats Keith Miller, Arthur Morris and Bill O'Reilly, playing against a local side.

They were training at the time in Townsville and the whole squad travelled to Cairns. Gold medallists Dawn Fraser, Lorraine Crapp and Ilsa and John Konrads were among those who competed. I played my first organised team sport in 1945-46 when Cairns State High allowed us to enter a team in the Cairns Cricket Association's C-grade competition. We used the school's gear but without coaching or organising help from teachers. Our training consisted of informal sessions during lunch breaks. Then in my first year in the workforce, I joined the Brothers club at the invitation of Fred Armbrust, a workmate at Mulgrave Shire Council who was captain of the club's B-grade team. We won the 1947-48 premiership. Teammates in that side included Jim Barlow, after whom Barlow Park was named, and Brian Bolton and Max Kelly, whom I rank as among the best cricketers this city has produced. Bolton was an exceptional talent and was still knocking out centuries in Cairns cricket at the age of 50. He would have held his own in any competition at grade level anywhere in the world.

Most cricket fixtures then were played at Norman (later Munro Martin) Park, Parramatta Park (Cairns Showground) and North Cairns reserve. No sporting organisation had thought of establishing its own ground, except the forward thinking Cairns Cricket Association.

The CCA in 1940 borrowed £500 (about $35,000 today) to buy 10ha of bushland in West Cairns that became cricket's headquarters. The CCA drew up plans for four cricket ovals, two full-size bowling greens, the foundations for which were laid in August 1950, tennis courts, children's playgrounds and pavilions. Clearing of the land began almost immediately once the purchase deal was sealed, but work was disrupted during World War II when it was occupied by the armed services. The ground may not have been developed but for the support of George Griffiths, after whom the ground was eventually named. Griffiths, a keen sportsman as a good all-round athlete, footballer and later a referee, cricketer, sailor and golfer, was better known as proprietor of Advanx Tyre & Motor Service, which traded at 61 Sheridan St as one of the city's three major motor dealers for more than half a century.

After the war, two grounds were levelled and top-dressed, concrete pitches laid, and a kiosk and gear pavilion was erected. A watering system was installed in 1948. At that time, Cairns was one of the few cricket associations outside of Brisbane to own its own playing fields. It was a brave decision by the CCA to develop the ground as I recall the Cairns and District Rugby League, at that time using Parramatta Park for its matches, was approached to become joint-owners. It declined because it was thought to be too far out of town to attract crowds.

The first match played at Griffiths Park was on Saturday, October 4, 1948, when Norths met Rovers. Jack Roberts, North's opening bat and manager of wines and spirits wholesale merchant Joseph Pease & Co, holds the distinction of facing the first ball bowled there by Charlie Tyson before going on to make 24, including the first six to be hit at the ground. Brothers wicketkeeper Bernie Mullins holds the other notable record for the ground, scoring the first century at Griffiths Park in November that year, including nine sixes in a typical hard-hitting innings.

I played a supporting role to that historic event. My good mate Brian Bolton and I, still in our teens, shared two partnerships with Bernie in Brothers' recovery against Norths from a dismal 5-70 to finish at 8-275 by stumps.

Players like Don Bradman, Stan McCabe, Jack Gregory, Alan Kippax, Warren Bardsley, Clarrie Grimmett and Don Tallon played in Cairns and other district centres in pre-World War II years. They travelled thousands of kilometres throughout NSW and Queensland country centres by rail and steamer, mostly at their own expense, so that people in remote areas could see players in action that otherwise they could only read about in newspapers.

In the match at Parramatta Park, Cairns, in 1931, locals were treated to Bradman at his best as he made 90 and 103 and took 4-13 and 6-43 with his medium-pacers. John Letson, the former finance director of *The Cairns Post*, wrote to Sir Donald Bradman with good wishes for his 86th birthday on August 27, 1994. John gave me a copy of Bradman's reply, in his own handwriting, in which he remembered his 1931 visit to play local teams. "Even at 86, I can remember playing in Cairns and planting a tree on the Atherton Tablelands where I think it still flourishes," he wrote. Bradman also planted the stand of royal palms that still grow tall today at the Ernest St

Keith Miller, the Australian cricketing great of the 1940s-50s, led a team of Sheffield Shield players to play in Cairns in 1956. Alan Hudson became acquainted with Miller when he was a regular visitor to Cairns in the 1980s working as a representative for Robert Sangster's Soccerpools.

end of Anzac Memorial Park, Innisfail, to commemorate his visit there in that same year.

The biggest crowd I have seen at Griffiths Park for a cricket match was in April 1952 when a Cairns side played a New South Wales team comprising some of Australia's leading players in Keith Miller, Arthur Morris, Bill O'Reilly, Jim De Courcey, Jack Moroney and Ray Flockton. This was the last of the teams of leading cricketers that once regularly visited country centres like Cairns. Keith Miller was popular on and off the field during that visit, as he was all over the world throughout his playing career. One of the special moments in my sporting life was meeting Miller later during my time as editor of *The Cairns Post*. I had always admired him as a role model for any young sportsperson. Miller once worked for Robert Sangster as his Australian representative for Soccerpools. He regularly called into my office at *The Cairns Post* when he was in the city to say hello, often with his former teammate Neil Harvey. Miller, flamboyant and debonair in his playing days, was charming but down to earth. On one of his visits, I had Raymond Andersen, a Mossman lad then in the first few weeks of his cadetship, interview Miller for a story for the paper. About four weeks later, Raymond, for years now the sports editor of the *Townsville Bulletin*, showed me a letter he had received from Miller. In his own handwriting on plain paper, Miller thanked Raymond for interviewing him, congratulated him on the article, and wished him well for his future in newspapers. This man, who had mixed with royalty and world leaders and usually had journalists and interviewers at his beck and all, had taken the trouble to write and encourage a young man in Far North Queensland embarking on a career in journalism. Is it any wonder that my admiration for Miller was greatly enhanced?

I also played my first competitive games of rugby league in 1947 when I joined Colts, a new club in Cairns, as a member of their 1947 minor junior (under-18) side with a few other local kids, including Ron Beecheno, Frank Gil and Joe Hickey. The club was disaffiliated after that one season as the Cairns District Rugby League wanted to avoid a bye with four-team competition of Gordonvale, Brothers, Ivanhoes and Kangaroos. Rugby league began in Cairns in August 1918 when rugby union handed over its assets to the new association. Matches were played at Norman Park before Parramatta Park became the headquarters for matches in 1927. I feel privileged to have played at a time when legends of the game like Jack Seary, Ralph Ross and Norm McHardie were still in the game.

Seary later became one of our top administrators, a CDRL president and founder of our junior rugby league association, while Ross for many years was a Queensland and Australian selector. McHardie, a lock forward, was the best footballer I played with or against. It still puzzles me how he was never chosen to play for Queensland. In later years Norm settled in Rockhampton but was a frequent visitor to Cairns as a racehorse trainer and licensed bookmaker. Playing in a Foley Shield final in Townsville in September was the ultimate aim

of all footballers in my time. Teams competed in the northern and southern zones for the right to meet on finals day in Townsville. The northern teams usually played one another twice for the Hanush Shield. Supporters gladly travelled long distances to follow their teams, usually by train. I remember playing in a Cairns side at Babinda in the early 1950s and two train services were needed to accommodate all of the players, officials and supporters who travelled to that game.

For Foley Shield final days in Townsville, a train usually left Cairns on Saturday about 9pm, reaching Townsville around dawn, then arriving back in Cairns at first light on Monday morning. Supporters were not afraid to back up their loyalty with hard cash. Individual bets of up to £100 (about $3000 today) on both club games and Hanush Shield matches were not unusual. Punters congregated before matches at Parramatta Park around the players' tunnel at the front of the Headrick grandstand to declare their bets. Tom Lysaght, a clerk in the railways in Cairns, was one of the big local punters. Tom always backed Brothers in club games and Cairns in representative matches.

Playing before the huge crowd at the Townsville Sports Reserve was a wonderful occasion when teams and supporters

The late Jack Seary, one of the legendary figures of rugby league in Cairns, was a senior player in the early 1950s when Alan Hudson made his debut in first grade.

The 1961 Eacham Foley Shield team led by captain coach John Eaton (seated second from right) was one of the district's best rugby league sides that Alan Hudson has seen.

from all over North Queensland gathered. I never did get to play in a Foley Shield final but I was a member of two Cairns under-20 sides which won the North Queensland title in 1949 and 1950. Both were exciting experiences that I will never forget, even though my on-field contribution in 1949 was cut short when I broke my collarbone during the match.

Eacham, Foley Shield winners in 1961 when led by former Queensland prop John Eaton and with the outstanding lock forward Jack Jones; Tully (1963) with Australian five-eighth Bob Banks at the helm and Angelo Crema (Australian second-rower) and Dan Clifford (Queensland forward) in the team; Innisfail (1960) with Australian second-rower Jim Paterson as captain-coach and again in 1964 and 1968 with Queensland centre Ron Tait as captain-coach and Australian winger Lionel Williamson in the side; and Cairns (1966) with Australian centre Alan Gil as captain and Queensland lock Stan Williams included, were some of the outstanding Foley Shield teams that I remember in the years when I followed the game closely. The expansion of the Cairns

District Rugby League, which started in 1980 to include other district teams from the Tablelands and south to Tully into a club competition, gradually eroded the prestige of the Foley Shield despite the best efforts of officials to maintain interest in the three-way competition between Cairns, Townsville and Mackay to this day.

In 1953, during my rugby league playing days with Brothers Football Club in Cairns, they introduced a bonus system as a tangible reward for senior players for their efforts. We did not win the premiership final, being pipped by penalty goal late in the match against Kangaroos. But at the end of that season we were ceremoniously handed over envelopes, with a handshake from the president, enclosing a short note thanking us for our performance and a cheque for £13 (about $400 today). Welcome to the age of professional sport.

Players of my generation often think back wistfully of that time in the context of today's age of professionalism when average NRL players earn up to $250,000 a year, backed by a coach and several assistants, various professional and medical staff, and rigged out in designer training gear and brand name clothes to wear to matches. When we played footy, we washed our own shorts and socks, trained twice a week after work, then usually retired to the nearest pub for six or eight beers. Players often helped most Friday nights selling raffle tickets in a meat tray around city hotels to raise money to support the club. We turned up on match day dressed in shorts and sandals (thongs had not been invented). Our support staff were a coach, who was often a paid player from the south, a manager who handed out guernseys, and a trainer who was an amateur masseur. In my time with Brothers, the trainer was an old fellow named Jock Young. Jock always carried a small port containing a grubby bath towel, a large roll of Elastoplast, pair of scissors and a bottle of acrid liniment, all of which he used to good effect to ready us for battle. No clubs had their own clubhouses, so after the game players and officials retired to the verandah of our local pub, or under a supporter's house, and shared a few beers well into the Sunday night. That was the sum total of our football week.

But I dare say we loved our rugby league as much, if not more, than today's professionals. I have often been asked how players of that era would cope with the professionalism of today's NRL. I am sure several would acquit themselves well, particularly someone like Frank Gil, the older brother of former Australian centre Alan. I could well imagine Frank, who was equally at home as fullback, centre or five-eighth, holding a place in any of today's NRL sides. He was an accurate goalkicker, safe handler, deadly tackler, and an astute leader. Frank has been an ornament to the game in Cairns for more than half a century, devoting countless hours of leisure time to coaching and administration.

The modern era has seen emerging sports introduced to Cairns that were unknown in my time, including endurance sports such as triathlon and mountain biking. Australian football, played as exhibition matches in the Cairns district by servicemen from Victoria during World War II, and basketball, two sports which now are regarded

Sam Leigh of Tinaroo Tigers handballs to a teammate in a match at North Cairns oval in 1958 soon after Australian football started in Cairns.

as among the city's most popular, had not even been thought of in my youth. Aussie rules had its start in Cairns in 1955 when Frank Vains, a former Victorian, and Bruce Muirden (ex-South Australia), two journalists working with him at *The Cairns Post*, had an item published inviting anyone with an Australian football background to have a social kick at North Cairns reserve the following Saturday afternoon.

Among the few who turned up were two ex-VFL players, Charlie Watts (Collingwood) and Kev Crathern (Richmond). Later that year Cairns played a team from Townsville for the Nielson Cup, which became the annual trophy contested by the two centres. On August 5, 1955 the inaugural meeting of the Cairns Australian National Football League took place in the Sea Scouts hall on the Esplanade. Souths became the league's foundation club in 1956 and a week later Norths joined. They played teams from Aloomba, Innisfail, Mossman and Tinaroo in those early times.

The late Kev Crathern was an old friend from the time we did battle in opposing teams in rugby league in the early 1950s, he with Ivanhoes and I with Brothers. When Kev and some of his ex-pat Victorian mates announced in 1957 they had purchased some land in Mulgrave Rd for £1225 (about $35,000 today) to develop as the future headquarters of Aussie rules in Cairns, I thought Kev had gone stark raving mad. The land they bought was largely a melaleuca swamp, habitable in the wet summer months only for wading birds, snakes and frogs.

That land today is the site of Cazaly's, one of Queensland's showpiece sporting grounds. It is a legacy of the great vision of those pioneers of the code, and an example of my appalling lack of the same commodity. Aussie rules was one of the few sports I never did tackle, but I watched with admiration as Kev Crathern and his mates toiled so hard to realise a dream where that former swamp has been the venue of several pre-season AFL matches and has hosted Test cricket.

Basketball had its first tentative start in Cairns in the early 1950s. I declined an invitation from some of my Brothers footy mates to become involved in non-competitive matches

Danny Morseu, Cairns's first male basketballer to play for Australia, has seen his sport make giant strides frrom the time it started here in the 1950s until today when the Taipans became the only national sporting team based in the city from the 1999-2000 season. Morseu suited up for St Kilda, Geelong and the Brisbane Bullets in the National Basketball League and represented Australia at the 1980 and 1984 Olympic Games.

at the Martyn St netball courts. The sport had its first real start when the Cairns Basketball Association was formed in 1958 with Graham Bruce as president. They played their matches at night on tennis courts in McLeod St and in 1960 moved to Mulgrave Rd to a site opposite Westcourt Plaza when up to 50 teams became involved. The present Aumuller St headquarters were occupied in 1961 when 121 teams were affiliated. The sport moved on in great leaps until 1999 when the Taipans became the first and only Cairns team to compete in a national competition when they were accepted into the National Basketball League. Cairns basketball, in its early years, produced two of this city's first national representatives in Rayleen Lynch and Danny Morseu. In 1967, Lynch became Queensland's first Queenlander, man or woman, to play basketball for Australia. She was a remarkably versatile athlete who holds the distinction of representing Australia in three separate sporting disciplines, playing for national teams in both softball and veterans' tennis. For good measure, she was also an outstanding golfer and was the Cairns Golf Club champion in 1991. Morseu was the first Cairns male basketballer to play for Australia, representing the country in both 1980 and 1984 Olympic Games. He also played for St Kilda, Geelong and the Brisbane Bullets in the NBL.

Hockey, in my memory, was the first sporting association to have encouraged junior talent in Cairns at a significant level when it moved into local schools to coach in the early 1950s and organised matches for youngsters. The sport, which began in the city in 1927, for many years has had the biggest enrolment of players with some 1200 registered at all levels. Hockey's Annette West will always rank highly in my ratings of the most outstanding athletes that Cairns has ever produced. She was a product of the local junior competition. Annette played for Queensland in 1966, then went to Canada to work and represented that country in 1968, and returned home to be selected for Australia from 1969 to 1974. After an all-nations tournament in New Zealand in 1971, sports writers named her in the key position of centre forward in their world team. There could be no higher accolade.

Racing has always been one of my favourite sporting activities dating back to my schooldays when I used to help a family friend, Jack von Nida, the brother of champion golfer Norman, with a magnificent black gelding named Cold Morn that he trained during World War II. There have been many highlights.

Younger racegoers could not appreciate how racing was conducted in pre-TAB days. Normal meetings at Cannon Park would attract up to 16 bookies betting on southern events, plus another 10 on the locals, and a busy, animated crowd of more than 1200 racegoers. Up to 60 bookmakers would operate on major meetings such as Cairns Cup day.

Veterans of the southern betting ring in Cairns included Joe Riddell, George Cannon, Sam Amies, Stan Allwood, Snowy Cox and Jerry Crowley. Jerry gave me my first part-time job in racing working in the SP shop he ran upstairs at 7-9 Shields St in partnership with Mike Speed. Younger guns in Roy Perrott, Vince Marsh, Jim Eustace, Herb Sang and George Lisha junior came later. Several bookies from out of town often fielded at Cairns and they included Phil Jue Sue, Bunny Allwood, Norm Davis (Tableland), George Hong, Mick Martin and Charlie Ah Shay (Innisfail). Among the regulars working on local races were Jimmy Brown, Con Cassimatis, George Tuckett, Roy Brewer, Tommy Goodwin, Arthur Best, George Chapman, Dick Conn and Roy Melvin.

Every small town in the Far North had at least one SP bookie. Police turned a blind eye to their operations and their occasional "raids", followed by token fines, were usually known in advance. Registered fielders operated some of the SP shops. Sam Amies had a shop at 141 Abbott St, just south of the City Library. Snowy Cox's was on the corner of Grafton and Shields streets opposite the Crown Hotel, and Bob Allwood's a few doors to the south of Snowy's in Grafton St at the rear of a billiards saloon. Joe Riddell and George Cannon ran one in partnership in the former Morrows biscuit factory which is now the bottle shop of the Crown Hotel. SP bookies operated on Friday night, up to noon Saturday when race meetings were held in Cairns, or all day when no local races were on. Bookmakers' clerks would have fond memories of those days. They were well paid and did not have the Taxation Department hassling them about their extra earnings. A few that I know paid off their mortgages or bought investment properties through the generosity of their Saturday employers. Some bookies paid their clerks handsomely on winning days. I know one clerk in the late 1950s who earned a minimum of £15 (worth about $450 today) for his Saturday job when his normal weekly wage was only about £20.

Several people who had their start in Cairns racing have gone on to achieve much bigger things in the south. H.F. (Fred) Best, who has been inducted into Queensland Racing's Hall of Fame for his dominance of Brisbane training ranks in the 1950s and 1960s, had his introduction to the sport in Cairns as a youngster. Ron Dillon, Gordon Franks and Clive Davis are among several others to have trained successfully in Brisbane after starting their racing careers in this city. Geoff Allendorf, who rode successfully in Sydney for some years and in recent times has been a prominent trainer in Macau, grew up in Cairns.

But the most successful of all has been Brian Mayfield-Smith who has trained horses for some of the world's most prominent owners over the past 20 years. I was one of his first owners when Brian started out as a trainer living in a caravan parked near his Cannon Park stables in 1971. We have remained good friends as the past three decades have taken him on a remarkable journey of success that included becoming Sydney's premier trainer for the 1985-86, when he ended a remarkable run of 32 successive premierships for the immortal Tommy Smith. He then won the premiership for the next two seasons. Brian stunned the racing world when he retired from training in 1995 and went to Africa with wife Maree to try to make a contribution to animal conservation.

He returned to Australia a year later and in 1997 set up as a trainer again at Flemington where he has had outstanding success with a relatively small team. Brian has never forgotten his roots or his old mates and on his last visit to

Leading Melbourne trainer Brian Mayfield-Smith began his career at Cairns in 1971 when he lived in a caravan at Cannon Park near his horses. Soon after moving to Sydney, he ended legendary trainer Tommy Smith's remarkable run of 32 successive titles by winning the first of his two successive premierships in 1985-86. In recent years he has had a relatively small team at his Flemington stables but is highly regarded for the winning strike rate with his gallopers.

Cairns for a short holiday he told me that his third placing with Maybe Better in the 2006 Melbourne Cup gave him one of his greatest thrills in racing.

Those of us who knew Frank Reys riding in pony races in Cairns in the 1940s could not have suspected we were watching a future Melbourne Cup winning jockey. Frank, one of 14 children of Filipino and Aboriginal heritage, graduated in 1949 from show-riding to apprentice jockey, indentured to Gordonvale trainer Alf Baker. Alf and Frank, with a galloper named Baysure, took off for Brisbane by rail in 1950 for a crack at the big time. Local racing men, being the cynics that they are, expected them back in quick time. But Frank stayed on, transferring his indentures to trainer Gordon Shelley and later linked up with wily veteran Alf Sands for a move to Sydney and later to Melbourne where Frank settled. With his riding talents and his innate courtesy and good manners, Frank soon became a respected member of the Melbourne racing industry, linking up with leading trainers Angus Armanasco and Ray Hutchins, who became a close friend.

Frank, aged 41 and the oldest jockey in the race, rode his way into racing history when he piloted Gala Supreme to victory in the 1973 Melbourne Cup, appropriately from the Hutchins stable. Frank's acceptance speech, during which he thanked family, friends and the horse's connections, was one

The late Frank Reys rode in gymkhanas and pony races in his home town of Cairns before making his debut as a jockey at Cannon Park. He achieved every jockey's dream when he won the 1973 Melbourne Cup on Gala Supreme.

of the longest and most emotional I have seen.

Frank almost quit race-riding due to a shocking run of falls and illness. It all started on October 19, 1972 when he suffered multiple injuries, requiring three major operations, in a race fall at Moe. Hutchins talked Frank out of retirement and they were rewarded with victory in the Melbourne Cup in what was regarded then as one of the finest riding performances in the history of the big race. Frank Reys died from cancer in 1984, aged 53.

Jack Wilson was a legendary figure of Cairns racing who did not leave the district to establish his formidable reputation as the best jockey I have seen from this city. Jack, who died in Cairns on September 20, 1997, aged 76, is believed to have ridden about 5000 winners in his career. One of his favourite horses was the former Melbourne galloper Zarook, who broke down after finishing eighth in the 1966 Caulfield Cup. Zarook was bought as a crock by Mt Molloy grazier Charlie Wallace and Mareeba-based trainer Dinko Pecotich nursed him back to health. In 1969 he won both the Townsville Cup and the North Queensland Cup, ridden by Jack Wilson. They then went to Brisbane where Zarook made a clean sweep of three

of Brisbane's feature races, the Brisbane Handicap (1600m), Queensland Cup (3200m) and the Recognition Stakes (2100m), a feat never performed before or since.

Racing has gone through many twists and turns since it started on a track just north of Edmonton and then became established at Cannon Park in July 1911. One of the most revolutionary changes ever proposed was a plan revealed in 2005 to sell the racecourse and build a new complex near Edmonton. The election of prominent Cairns developer Tom Hedley at the Cairns Jockey Club annual general meeting in December 2006 saw those plans scrapped. Hedley has since led a remarkable resurgence of interest in local racing and an upgrading of facilities at Cannon Park that seems to have assured racing's future in Cairns.

I attended a race meeting at Cannon Park on September 18, 1959 never dreaming it would one day become one of Australia's major sporting and social events known simply as the Cairns Amateurs. When it was proposed, the Far North Queensland Amateur Turf Club based its plans on the historical Oak Park races as a way of bringing city and country together. It was the brainchild of Sir Sydney Williams and Les Gallagher, who owned the Imperial Hotel in Cairns at the time. The first president was Ken Atkinson who served from 1959 until 1964 when Syd Williams took the position. In 2001, Sir Sydney stood down and Alan McPherson succeeded him. Only amateur jockeys were allowed to ride until many years later when professionals took over.

By the 1970s, visitors from all over Australia and overseas flocked to the region and stayed for the carnival. Over the years, southern race callers such as Keith Noud and Wayne Wilson attended as guest commentators. The committee arranged not just a race meeting, but a full week of activities, highlighted by the now traditional club dinner on the Friday night held then, and for the next 20 years, at George Cannon's White Rock residence. The week fulfilled the foundation members' aim of getting country and city people together socially. It would take a separate book to write about the many highlights I have seen in the history of the Amateurs.

Brian Mayfield-Smith won a double at the 1971 Amateurs in his first year as a trainer with Grenoble Boy and Quran. Brian will say today that Grenoble Boy's success still ranks as one of his most satisfying training achievements. The gelding, owned by Cooktown publican Col Rowbotham, had a limited preparation because of unsound legs, yet he led for most of

the 2000m journey at the juicy odds of 14-1.

The best riding performance I have seen anywhere, and one that most likely will never be equalled, was the astonishing effort by the Hughenden-based slaughterman, Graham (Nobby) Cairns, in winning on all eight of his mounts (five on the first day) at the Cairns Amateurs in 1972, including the feature race on both programs. Punters used to say that it was a waste of time studying form when they could simply back Nobby's mounts and show a profit. His effort was all the more meritorious as he competed against some of the best amateur riders that I have seen in this area, including Charlie Prow, Lyle O'Neill, Noel Thomson, Alan Atkinson, Ron Thompson and Terry Kane.

It is every owner's ambition to win a race at the Cairns Amateurs and one of my treasured memories is the success I enjoyed on the first day of the 1983 meeting. Roman Candle, a gelding that I raced in Brisbane as partner with my great friend Cam Boyle of Caloundra, and our Murgon mates Bill Roberts and Lee Burton, won the main race, the Carlton United Cup (1400m), in record time. We helped ourselves to the lucrative odds after bookies bet as much as 33-1. Graham Purdy, a successful Tablelands trainer for many years, rode the horse to victory for us.

The saddling enclosure at Cannon Park racecourse, not many years after the Cairns Mulgrave Jockey Club held its first meeting at the course on July 4, 1911.

The Cairns Post started its life in a wooden building in Lake St where the Palace budget accommodation complex is today. It moved to this new reinforcecd concrete building with its four Ionic columns at 22 Abbott St in 1908. Extensions to the adjoining southern site added five more columns, with work completed in 1926. Management made a decision to install electric light and power from the new city supply, replacing a gas engine plant. *The Cairns Post* was the first building in Cairns to use Ionic columns. Others to follow were Cairns City Council (now City Library), Public Curator's Offices (now Cairns Regional Gallery), former Cairns Courthouse (now Courthouse Bar) and Cairns State High School.

Chapter six - 1970s

I started reading *The Cairns Post* as a child when my mother dragged me from my bed around 6.15am every day to walk up to Apps's shop in Bunda St and buy the paper and milk for breakfast. The paper had classified advertisements covering the front page and it once cost twopence. What a proud day it was for me in May 1974 when I was appointed editor of the newspaper that had been part of my life for so long. While it was a privilege to serve in that position for more than 17 years, it was even more exciting to have been involved in the most amazing changes in a single decade that had ever taken place in the industry.

The Cairns Post observes 1882 as its foundation year, although the first newspaper under that name was not published until May 10, 1883 from rough timber premises in Lake St (about No. 86). F.T. (Fred) Wimble founded the *Post* as a weekly newspaper until 1888 and it was then twice a week until 1893. Wimble invested heavily locally in land, businesses and the sugar industry, and lost everything in a bank crash of 1893. The newspaper regarded as the most direct ancestor of *The Cairns Post* was *The Cairns Morning Post*. It first appeared on June 6, 1895, founded by E. Draper and Company. It became a daily in 1904 and continued until 1909 when its name reverted to *The Cairns Post*.

In 1908, the present building, with only four columns and single-storeyed, was constructed at 22 Abbott St. Additions were made and five columns added after an adjoining wooden building was demolished in the mid-1920s. A.J. Draper, known as "The Father of Cairns" because of his prominence in business and civic affairs, was registered as managing director on October 4, 1913. The newspaper was still owned and controlled by the Draper family until November 26, 1965, when bought by Queensland Press Ltd, publishers of

Linotype operators in *The Cairns Post's* composing room in the 1970s set type for the newspaper under the old hot-metal system. A new computerised operation was installed in 1978.

The Cairns Post journalists, with Paddy Hintz (seated), Gail Sedorkin and Debra McCoy in the foreground, welcomed the major renovations to their working environment in the 1980s after the introduction of computerisation. The editorial department then occupied the western part of the second level of the building.

The Courier-Mail. On May 1, 1978, the first of the changes into the modern era of newspaper publishing was introduced when *The Cairns Post* became the first in Australia to switch from the old hot metal production to the cold-type computerised photographic process. *The Cairns Post* changed from broadsheet to its present tabloid format on July 1, 1986 when it installed a modern new Uniman press at its Dutton St works. The familiar titlepiece in elegant Old English typeface was changed to a new colourful masthead. I spent many hours before my retirement in July 1991 redesigning the paper, which included another new masthead which appears at the top of the paper today. The *Post* became part of Rupert Murdoch's News Limited group in January 1987.

All departments were under the same roof at 22 Abbott St until July 1986. The press room, which was moved in 1986 to Dutton St, advertising and administration, commercial printing section and stationery retail shop were on the ground floor, with the editorial and composing room for printers working on the newspaper side on the second floor.

Journalists today are accommodated in modern and spacious airconditioned offices seated at ergonomically designed work stations. But editorial offices when I arrived at the *Post* in January 1969 were largely unchanged from an earlier age. Paint peeled from ceilings and walls, and floor coverings were cracked and curling at the edges. With no airconditioning, offices were draughty and cold in winter and steaming hot in summer, relieved only by a gentle breeze from a lonely fan.

Like a scene from a Dickens novel, some sub-editors still wore eyeshades as they worked in the dimly lit rooms. They marked their copy seated at tiny desks stacked with paper and pots of paste, while reporters tapped out stories on clapped out old typewriters, usually castoffs from downstairs offices. Journalists worked in several little rooms, one each for the editor and chief sub-editor, another for the social reporter, a cadet whose specialty was debutante balls, and two others for newspaper files and a teletype machine which clattered away at a pedestrian pace to bring us news from other parts of the world. Sub-editors and reporters worked in a slightly larger common room.

When I took over the newspaper in May 1974, editorial staff totalled 13, including the editor, with no clerical support (when I retired in July 1991, *The Cairns Post* employed some 34 journalists). The other 12 staffers in early days handled all sub-editing and reporting, including sport. Sports pages were laid out by staff on general sub-editing shifts. The only sport covered directly was rugby league and racing. Before my time, reporters were simply assigned to "rounds" with little direction, largely left to their own initiative as what to cover, apart from regular events like police and courts, and meetings of councils, ambulance committee and Cairns Chamber of Commerce that were specifically assigned.

News coverage of regional areas until then had been through a network of correspondents and by telephone from our Abbott St offices. Every evening soon after starting the night shift at 6pm, a reporter would work through a list of telephone rounds to the police, ambulance and fire brigade in a dozen or more towns throughout the region.

The reporter called Cairns telephone exchange, then operated manually. They had an identical list, and calls were connected in order. In that way we received news of fires, motor vehicle accidents, criminal activity, other incidents and court reports. Wives of many officers knew the procedure and often provided us with information if their husbands were away on call.

Our network of about 15 part-time correspondents included regulars who were institutions in their communities like Mena Fallon and Nell Trainor (Innisfail), Janet Crump (Herberton), Doreen McGrath (Petford) and Gwen Moloney (Thursday Island). They sent in reports, either typewritten or neatly composed by hand. They arrived by mail on a regular basis, either weekly or monthly. Correspondents claimed payment at an agreed rate. It was once a penny per published line. Reports from smaller centres were largely on social happenings, such as CWA meetings or interesting visitors to their area. A debutante ball was a major event. A student home on holidays from boarding school or someone who had spent a day in Cairns shopping might be worth a paragraph.

Editor Alan Hudson supervised several major changes to *The Cairns Post* through the 1970s and '80s, but two that ruffled the feathers of readers were replacing classified advertisements on the back page that was headed by funeral notices with sport in the late 1970s, and conversion from the old broadsheet to what was perceived as a "flippant and racy" tabloid format from July 1, 1986.

Some correspondents had never met the editor or even spoken to a staffer by telephone. I drove to their towns to meet them on their own turf, and tried to encourage some to produce more "hard" news, rather than just social jottings. I asked one woman to attend the weekly magistrate's court and telephone us with details of more interesting cases. "Oh, I couldn't do that," she said. "I have to live with these people."

Our own reporters went to regional centres only rarely for major events. The annual district RSL conference was a favourite. They then had to drive back to the office to type out their stories or telephone them through to another reporter. I remember covering a Foley Shield rugby league match in Ingham around 1970. I read my copy back to the office from a public telephone box alongside the main highway, with rain pelting down so heavily I could barely make myself heard. I eventually convinced our money-managers to make an investment in regional coverage and we appointed a resident reporter in Innisfail and on the Tablelands. Duncan Paterson and Leslene Woodward filled those positions capably for many years and our coverage of councils and other current news from those areas improved significantly.

Adjusting to new technology from the late 1970s was often stressful for reporters and printers used to functioning under a system that had been in place for a century or more. A few older printers found the change too difficult to adjust to and opted for retirement. The first major change to the newspaper's format was conversion from the age-old hot metal method to computerised typesetting on May 1, 1978.

Wire service news then fed into our computer instead of being sent by teleprinter. We redesigned the paper's format so that it was more sectionalised with regular features like finance news, letters, and other services in the same place every edition. The biggest change was relocation of sport from inside pages to the back page. Until then we had classified advertisements on the back page. There was a general outcry from readers: "We can't find the funeral notices". Until then the last column of the back page was headed by funerals, births and engagements. They soon became used to the new procedure.

The next time we ruffled the feathers of readers was on July 1, 1986 when we changed from the old broadsheet format to tabloid with installation of a new hi-tech computerised printing press, the first of its kind to be used by a newspaper in the Southern Hemisphere. It was part of a $7 million upgrade of the newspaper. From that first edition, a perception by many readers that broadsheet meant serious and respected, while tabloid was flippant and racy, was difficult to overcome. I remember speaking later to Mrs Dawn Walker, daughter of Arthur H. Clarke, one of the city's first stockbrokers when the Cairns Stock Exchange was set up during the boom mining years of the early 1900s when there were 20 stockbrokers in Cairns. Mrs Walker told me how her first reaction to the new tabloid paper was one of shock. "It might have been the colour, but I was annoyed and unhappy," she said. "I thought the paper had lost its dignity. But I was like many readers, clinging to the familiar old newspaper we had grown up with. After I got used to it, I thought it was great." The Cairns Chamber of Commerce even complained that we were publishing less overseas news. On many occasions I sat down with people to convince them *Post* staffers were the same who had published the old broadsheet paper, and certainly we had not changed our policy on news coverage and presentation. We gradually won them over.

Memories of an earlier age for former linotype operators John Sands, Syd Shellback and Ray Thompson as they inspect the last edition's type set under the old hot metal system that was replaced by computerisation at *The Cairns Post* in 1978.

The Cairns Post did not employ staff photographers until the late 1980s. Commercial photographers took news pictures on assignment. If a fire, vehicle smash, or other mishap happened we had to hope someone would be readily available. We did not even have picturegram facilities to receive images from our Brisbane office. If we wanted to publish a photo of some national or overseas event, it was sent by air freight, arriving in Cairns around 8.30pm. Brisbane sent us an advisory of photos with vertical or horizontal format so we could draw them into our page design in advance. A journalist waited patiently outside Ansett's Lake St office after 8.30pm for the prized package. Too often we planned to run a picture on our main news pages only to find our packet had been offloaded in Townsville or another airport for reasons we could never establish.

Installation of the new press in July 1986 allowed us to publish colour photos. However, we had no staff trained to process colour separations for more than a year. They were sent to Brisbane with a four-day turnaround. I decided we had to avail ourselves of the new facility, so we planned in advance to use lifestyle scenes like garden shows or anniversary celebrations and major sporting events. We "dummied" the scenario for a photo session, sent the transparency or colour print to Brisbane by airfreight on Monday and had the separations back by Thursday night to run the photo on our front page on Saturday.

Our first colour photo appeared on the front page of the new tabloid paper on July 2, 1986. It showed Clare MacKenzie, a Cairns State High School senior, switching on our new press. Clare, who later worked for us as a cadet journalist, had won the honour in an essay competition held in all district schools. The photo was actually taken about 10 days before. We were careful that Clare on the night she actually switched on the press wore the same dress and other adornments and had her hair styled the same way. We had a dinner party at the Pacific International for civic leaders and other local business people that night to celebrate the occasion. At about 11pm, we distributed an early edition

Publishing a photo in processed colour of the explosion at the gas works in Bunda St in the August 16, 1987 edition provided editorial and production staff of *The Cairns Post* with one of their greatest challenges.

of the new tabloid newspaper to diners with the front page colour photo and other photos and stories on inside pages of the ceremony at the press room that they had attended a few hours previously. We regarded it as quite a coup for both production and editorial staff.

A major test of our resourcefulness came when a massive explosion at the Bunda St gasworks on the afternoon of August 15, 1987 killed a man and caused massive damage in the vicinity. Commercial photographers had taken many shots in the aftermath. Several members of the public offered us rolls of film of shots they had taken. We arranged with Cec Turner, who owned McBride's Pharmacy across the road from our Abbott St offices, to process all films as priority.

As I inspected the pictures with senior staff, one of the dozens of images virtually jumped out at us. A Holloways Beach man named Jim Hendry had captured the spectacular fireball scene seconds after the major explosion. It would have to be used, though, in black and white. What a pity. But our production manager Peter Carthew asked the late Bob Bolton, owner of G.K. Bolton Printers, whose premises were then in McLeod St near the Spence St corner, if he could

Two hundred riders and their mounts approach Cairns through Brinsmead on October 9, 1976 at the end of their four-day trail ride which traced the original track from the Hodgkinson goldfields to Trinity Bay to celebrate the city's centenary.

Picture: Gordon Markey

help. It was close to knock-off time at 5pm. "Yes, I'd be glad to help," said Bob. "But my man who does our separations is playing indoor hockey tonight and he'll do them when he finishes the game (around 9pm)." And he did.

We had many anxious moments before the separations were ready for us late that night. The gas explosion on the front page of our August 16, 1987 edition was the first colour photo of a major news event that *The Cairns Post* published. In the months ahead, Jim Hendry sold dozens of prints of that photo to magazines and trade publications throughout Australia and overseas.

Since my retirement as editor in July 1991, technological changes have taken place at an astonishing rate. Rapid advances in information technology over the past decade or so have been mind-boggling for old journalists who were brought up in the days of notebooks, typewriters, copy paper and pots of paste. The printing department and its typesetters and compositors, an integral part of newspapers for centuries, have become redundant. Sub-editors for years now have been able to compose complete pages on the screens of their computer terminals, scanning in photos and graphics. Information and images are instantly available from all over the world by tapping out a few commands on a computer keyboard, within minutes of a news event taking place.

The 1970s were a time when the settled image of the old Cairns started to change appreciably. The city's first home for the aged opened, the Royal Flying Doctor Service established a base here, HMAS Cairns naval base was commissioned, the new Cairns Civic Centre was opened, our first suburban shopping centre opened at Raintrees, extensive flood mitigation continued and our homes received water from the new Copperlode Dam.

The steady growth of Cairns saw development of outer suburbs that were bush only a decade or so earlier, or occupied by dairies and sugar cane farms. Townships like Gordonvale and Edmonton in the south, and Stratford,

Freshwater and Redlynch in the north, were virtually self-sufficient, with their own pubs, shops, schools, post office and other facilities. Few of their residents had a need to come into the city and rarely did. Long-time residents remember the beaches to the north only as places to visit for Sunday outings. Some did not even have a listing in the telephone directory. But they, and other formerly small communities at Machans Beach, Holloways Beach, Yorkeys Knob, Trinity Beach, Kewarra Beach, Clifton Beach and Palm Cove, were gradually claimed as part of Cairns suburbia.

The highlight of the decade came in 1976 when Cairns held its biggest-ever celebration to commemorate the city's centenary. A huge calendar throughout the year of 100 major events, including conferences and seminars, and sporting, social and cultural activities, was organised by a huge committee of prominent Cairns people, headed by Bob (later Sir Robert) Norman.

They began with a Turn of the Century Ball on New Year's Eve starting on December 31, 1975 and ending the next morning with a torch lighting ceremony. The main events of the year's program were the Centennial Trail Ride from the Hodgkinson goldfields to Cairns, following roughly the trail from the inland goldfields that was forged back in 1876 to lead to the settlement of Cairns, and the Centenary Cavalcade on Saturday, October 9, 1976, 100 years to the day after the first settlers arrived in Trinity Bay.

More than 200 riders from New Zealand, South Australia, Victoria and Queensland took part in the four-day 150km trail ride. It ended in spectacular fashion at 4.45pm on Friday, October 8, 1976 when huge crowds lined the CBD streets to welcome the riders who brought eight sacks of mail containing 10,000 commemorative letters carried from Thornborough to be delivered to the Cairns post office in Abbott St. They were handed to postal workers dressed in the fashion of waistcoats and eyeshades popular in the city's early days. Thousands of people took part in the centenary cavalcade in Cairns the next afternoon when 160 floats took part in a procession.

City streets awash with water were a regular occurrence during the wet season in the early part of my life. Old-time residents often remark, "We don't get the wet seasons like we used to in the old days." Cairns may have an average annual rainfall of about 2000mm, but that does not support such a sweeping statement. Cairns City Council embarked upon an extensive program of flood mitigation into the 1970s. Floodwaters now run off more quickly with a better drainage system and, because we do not see the spectacular flooding we had half a century ago, we are inclined to believe the wet is not quite as wet as it used to be.

People were rowing boats around flooded Cairns streets as far back as March 1911. The last of no fewer than three tropical cyclones that summer dumped in three days up to 1800mm of rain, nearly half the annual total, in one of the wettest years on record. It seems that almost every summer in my younger days there was heavy flooding somewhere in city. I recall walking to Parramatta State School from Buchan St in the late 1930s, wading up to my thighs through floodwaters rushing across Mulgrave Rd where the Fearnley St drain is today. My family once lived on the ground floor of a two-storey house in Bunda St that had 15cm of water running through it for several days in the late 1940s.

The Cairns Post of March 30, 1949 reported that the previous day brought "the worst flooding to the inner city business area since the disastrous 1927 cyclone". "The whole city is awash with up to 9 inches (23cm) of water along footpaths outside some shops," the report said. "At Kennedy's corner (opposite the council chambers) about 1pm, a group of children returning to school (after lunch) were cut off by the raging torrent sweeping feet-deep down the gutter and across the footpath. They eventually managed to cross by holding hands and forming chains."

I remember once seeing a vehicle from F.R. Irelands towing a car that had stalled in knee-deep floodwaters in Lake St, just outside the School of Arts (now Cairns Museum). *The Cairns Post* on January 15, 1951 reported that a downpour of 760mm in less than five hours had caused landslides and closed the Cook Highway north of Buchan Point. "Gigantic trees were uprooted and ground to pulp and boulders as high as 10 feet (3m) were hurled into the Pacific as though they were marbles," the report said.

Older residents would remember early in 1974 when Reg Holtz hoodwinked *The Cairns Post* into publishing a photo of a fish he had "caught" from a rowboat in floodwaters between the Grand Hotel and Railway Hotel at the western end of Shields St. Reg, proprietor of the Railway Newsagency in Shields St next door to the Railway Hotel, had dangled a lifelike (but plastic) fish from the end of his fishing rod and the photo, taken by professional photographer John Pesch, was convincing enough for *Post* editor Reg Sutton to accept it as being the real thing.

Graeme Haussmann, city engineer from 1959-88, once told me about a night early in January 1964, when he walked through floodwaters from the rear entrance of council chambers down Lake St to Boland's corner where the water, flowing down Spence St to escape over the Esplanade's sea wall, was almost up to his knees. The ground floor of Boland's was flooded. That kind of flooding was no surprise. The rain was so heavy that 200mm was recorded in 85 minutes around midnight. "There was no soakage then," Graeme said. "Now there are underground drains to take floodwaters away."

The first serious attempt to drain the city's swamps had been in World War II when a series of small open drains were constructed to prevent pondage during the wet season as part of a government-subsidised anti-malarial campaign. Major flood mitigation works began in the 1960s when the city's drainage system was designed and they continued into the 1970s. New drains were built in the flood-prone residential suburbs and others widened. A 1m pipe once drained the whole Pease St area. Now the watercourse is so wide that people fish there and it flows under a large traffic bridge. Reclamation of Alligator Creek in 1963-64 and construction of the Fearnley St drain also provided a more efficient flow of floodwaters out of the area.

Shoppers wade through floodwaters in the main CBD area of Abbott St opposite *The Cairns Post* in the 1950s before major flood mitigation works in later years eased the problem.

It was not unusual for CBD streets to be flooded during heavy rain in Cairns before better drainage and other flood mitigation works were undertaken. Pictured after a heavy downpour in 1958 (from left) are Lillian Faithfull, Violet Holtz and Hazel Heaslop, who were employed in Reg Holtz's Railway Newsagency, next door to the Railway Hotel in Shields St.

Picture: Cairns Historical Society

The opening in 1974 of Farnorha in Westcourt, the city's first home for the aged, came about through one of the best grassroots community efforts I have seen in Cairns in my lifetime. (The name of Farnorha, often spelled incorrectly, is a combination of the "Farnor" from Far North, then the "h" for home and "a" for aged).

Some 40 years ago, I met an American town planner visiting Cairns for a conference. He told me one of our city's more important planning issues was not roads, water or any other type of conventional municipal infrastructure, but catering to the future needs of our aged and infirm. "People will be living longer and if you don't start planning now, you'll be running into serious problems by the year 2000," he told me. When this need became obvious in Cairns, people from all walks of life rallied to the cause and the response was quite remarkable.

The genesis for what became our Farnorha home for the aged was an offer in the 1950s of a parcel of land in West Cairns facing Lyons and Mann streets to G.W.G. (Watty) Wallace, a former city alderman who was also our family butcher, working from a shop at 153 Bunda St.

Wallace, who was then the Labor member for Cairns, asked Cairns mayor Bill Fulton to call a public meeting to discuss the possibility of building a home for the aged, using land offered by an anonymous donor who, it later transpired, was the La Cava family. "People of Cairns have a duty to do something in regard to the aged," Wallace said.

About 45 people attended the meeting at the Cairns City Council chambers on July 28, 1959, and resolved to form a citizens steering committee with a view to building a home for the aged. It comprised Darcy Chataway, Graeme Haussmann, Dr Charles Knott, Doug Watkins, Allan McInnes, Rev. E.L. Scarlett, Watty Wallace, with Les Williams (secretary) and Cec Williams (town clerk) as secretary.

Farnorha Aged Home committee and volunteers at the opening of the first stage of Farnorha on September 10, 1972. Member for Leichhardt and former Cairns mayor Bill Fulton and his wife Thelma are seated (centre). On Fulton's left is Basil Creedy, long-serving president of the committee, and next to him Cairns Pensioners League president Phil Penny and his wife Myna.

The Commonwealth Bank, on the corner of Abbott and Spence streets, was one of the city's first. It was established in the early 1900s as the Queensland Government Savings Bank. The Commonwealth took it over in 1921 and erected a new building, adding extensions in the 1930s and 1950s. It remained there until after the bank moved in 1973 to its present premises in Lake St.

One of the first decisions the committee made was to appoint Frank La Cava as life governor. The first fund for the new home was a modest donation of one guinea (about $30 today) by the Cairns Pensioners League. By mid-1965, the land had been cleared and a large sign erected that said: "Far Northern Home for the Aged". A foundation stone was laid on November 21, 1971; the first 18 residents entered the home on May 27, 1972; and the official opening was on September 10, 1972. By March 1980, 13 buildings at Farnorha housed 70 citizens, with the complex valued at a conservative $1 million (today about $9 million).

And not one cent was owing on it. That brief statement indicates what a wonderful achievement it was, but it does not adequately convey the extraordinary community effort that went into its establishment, nor the wonderful contribution by so many individuals. Literally dozens of Cairns people became involved in one of the greatest fund-raising efforts this city has seen. The support came from all-corners in the region. Families made substantial donations, garden parties, fashion parades, raffles and art unions (one in 1966 for a home at Yorkeys Knob) were held to raise funds, pubs took up collections, door-knocks were held and service and sporting clubs chipped in with generous donations.

If accolades were to be handed out, where would one begin? Frank La Cava would have to be given prime consideration for donating the land, earthmoving contractor Ted Tanner for clearing it, city engineer and member of the steering committee Graeme Haussmann for valuable advice on costs and feasibility use of the site.

Then there were Basil Creedy, former champion footballer and lawn bowler and deputy mayor of Cairns, for chairing the committee for many years and doing more than his share of volunteer work, and Cairns businessman Dave Chaplain who succeeded Basil in the chair. There were many other stalwarts of the 16-person committee, some of whom I did not know, like Gwen Hart who was treasurer for 20 years. No account of the early days of Farnorha would be complete without mention of architect partners, Don Channer and

George James, who prepared the drawings for the buildings, with Channer also serving on the committee as well. Percy Woods, a local bottle merchant I knew who had a heart as big as Phar Lap, served on the committee, and I remember him rounding up some of his Labor Party mates to sell raffle tickets and accompany him on door-knock appeals for funds. Percy also put his hand up when Farnorha was built to take on responsibility for ground maintenance. Ross Wintour, who was a driving force behind road safety in the Cairns region for many years, was secretary for several terms.

But my favourite volunteers were the retirees who operated two city car-parking areas with all proceeds going towards the home. They raised more than $80,000 (worth at least $250,000 today) in the 13 years up to 1980, and to put that amount into perspective, you could park your car for the whole of the working week for $1 in the early days. This move that provided the real impetus for fund-raising came from Adam Paterson, who approached Carlton and United Breweries Ltd for use of the vacant lot on the corner of Spence St and the Esplanade for use as car parking.

CUB agreed and the lot where the Strand Hotel and adjoining Ansett offices became a city car park in 1967. I used to park my car there and well remember being greeted by the cheerful presence of the volunteers, including Basil Creedy, Phil Penny, Jim McGowan and Horrie Eyles. A second park was run by the Farnorha volunteers in Lake St, where the National Mutual building is today.

I remember how September 10, 1972 was a gala day for Cairns and a proud one for the Farnorha committee, the dozens of volunteers and the community as a whole. The first five lodges carried the names of great supporters of the home: Frank La Cava who donated the land, Watty Wallace who arranged the first public meeting and continued his support for the project and Phil Penny, president of the Cairns Pensioners League, who gave so much of his time with his wife, Myna, to raising funds. Two other lodges were named after gentlemen I did not know: Messrs Ellis and Ainscow who had left money for Legacy widows.

The city library, now housed in the former council chambers in Abbott St, went into Cairns City Council control in 1979. The original library was located in the School of Arts building in Lake St, which now houses the Cairns Museum. I remember going there in the 1950s and the reading room and shelves of books, modern by standards of those days, were like a scene from a bygone age. It was well-patronised, and there always seemed to be men taking part in the board games located on the verandah section where the Chess Club activities were revived in 1953.

The woman who contributed so much to the library was the secretary/librarian, Mrs Mary O. ("Shan") Walmsley, who held the position from 1949 until 1973. She was the wife of Murray Walmsley, a former partner in a Lake St accountancy firm, Kerr Walmsley & Co, who also served as an alderman on the Cairns City Council. Although she was appointed late in 1948 initially as a book-mender, Shan Walmsley was a qualified librarian who worked for the American services library in Longreach during World War II. She was appointed as secretary/librarian when the position was vacated by the resignation of Miss Dawn Huddy.

The library, which began in 1887 with 400 books, had taken on a resurgence from the 1930s, but declined during World War II when a Cairns branch of the Red Cross was accommodated in the building. Books in the library until then had been mainly fiction, but Mrs Walmsley quickly introduced a program of expansion. She had previously visited Brisbane and Sydney and had purchased 450 new books, mainly non-fiction and reference titles. She upgraded the junior section and brought in hundreds of books of non-fiction, and Cairns soon became known as one of the best reference libraries outside of Brisbane with encyclopaedias and titles on arts, crafts, music, travel, boat-building, sport and all sorts of hobbies imaginable.

It was purchasing 1000 books a year from 1950 on, and had 40,000 titles on its shelves when it ceased operating on those premises in 1977. It had 1000 subscribers in 1949. The School of Arts Library in 1953 was registered as a training

The city's library once operated in the School of Arts building, now the Cairns Museum in the City Place. It was taken under Cairns City Council control and moved to a new building in 1974 on the site formerly occupied by F.R. Ireland, car dealer.

institution for trainee librarians. A travelling library service was provided for senior citizens, and a country borrowers service was also introduced to embrace the area between Cairns, Mt Isa, Normanton and Thursday Island. One of the lasting initiatives was the formation in 1946 of the Cairns Historical Society which still operates from the premises.

Cairns was barely 10 years old when Fred T. Wimble, part-owner and editor of *The Cairns Post* proposed the establishment of the School of Arts. Wimble was the first to put his hand in his pocket and donated 10 guineas to a subscription list, and his move was quickly followed by Mr McColl, owner of Hides Hotel, and Dan Patience, manager of Burns Philp & Co. and later to serve as mayor. The School of Arts began as a reading room on Christmas Eve 1885 with its library opening in 1887 when it was well supplied with English and colonial newspapers. It was opened to borrowers

on March 3, 1887. In those days before government sponsored adult education and TAFE colleges, the School of Arts supported many other activities, including a Literary and Debating Society that began in 1889. Shorthand classes, drawing and bookkeeping were added in 1893, painting in 1905, and millinery and machine drawing and design in 1908. The Education Department took over full management of these adult education classes in 1911 and still functioned in the building until 1923.

The School of Arts closed its doors on June 30, 1977 and the assets were transferred to the Cairns City Council with a new library opening in February 1979 in Lake St where F.R. Ireland & Co. operated before moving to Mulgrave Rd. The present library, in the old council chambers in Abbott St, began operating in 1999. It has seven other branch libraries in the city's jurisdiction.

Queensland Governor Sir Leslie Orme Wilson (foreground) and mayor Billy Collins (second from left) inspect the major augmentation of Cairns's water supply at Crystal Cascades in 1935. The city's first piped supply began on August 5, 1911 gravitating from a reservoir at Freshwater Creek.

Lake Morris, the great expanse of water behind Copperlode Dam, was deservedly named after the former long-serving city engineer Frank Roland Morris, who identified the site in the late 1930s to ensure the city's water supply into the future.

Lake Morris, the expanse of water over an area of about 350ha behind Copperlode Dam, is a significant and important part of this city's infrastructure. It was the third and most recent of the major schemes to ensure a reliable supply of water for this city. It was appropriate that the area should have been named after former city engineer Frank Roland Morris, a quiet, forward-thinking man who first identified the Copperlode site for Cairns's future water supply as far back as the late 1930s. However, no money was available for the scheme then and conventional wisdom at the time was that the city's needs were being well met for the foreseeable future.

Cairns's first water reticulation system tapping into Freshwater Creek was officially opened on August 5, 1911. From the time of settlement in 1876 until then, the people of Cairns drew their supplies of water from corrugated rainwater tanks that every home in Cairns had during my childhood, or by sinking shallow wells and putting down spears in the low sand ridges on which our city was built.

The Freshwater scheme had been in the planning stage from the time in July 1892 when the state government's hydraulic engineer J.B. Henderson submitted his first report, indicating that Freshwater Creek was the most promising of several possible sources. But it took years before the scheme was implemented with the intake at Freshwater Creek about 100m above sea level, and the main pipeline running through a short tunnel in the hill behind Freshwater. The line crossed Freshwater Creek four times.

Construction was difficult as the first couple of kilometres through dense tropical jungle were so rough that road transport was impracticable and pipes had to be handled by means of a 2ft (60cm) tramline using horse-drawn sleds. Locals attended the grand opening in Abbott St, opposite the old Imperial Hotel on the corner of Shields St, when the Cairns Fire Brigade tested the water pressure after it had been officially opened by the wife of the mayor, John Hoare.

Apart from household use, among other advantages of Cairns's first reticulated water supply were that fire hoses were able to be used regularly to water the streets to lay the dust, and water-driven fans were put into use in many of the town's offices during the summer months. A separate water board was set up to administer the new supply with its first meeting held on July 27, 1911. As the population grew and demand increased, two additional augmentations of the Freshwater supply took place, the first in 1927 at Crystal Cascades, and the second above Crystal Cascades in 1933.

By the mid-1940s, Frank Morris and Mulgrave shire engineer Reg Rudge began planning the Behana Creek scheme and it was the catalyst for the formation of the Cairns Mulgrave Water Supply Board in 1946. Town clerk Cecil Williams, the former Mulgrave shire clerk, later described the project as the largest job to be undertaken in North Queensland next to the Tully Falls Hydro Electric scheme.

It would augment supply to Cairns and northern suburbs of Stratford, Freshwater and Redlynch, provide a new gravitation system for Gordonvale as well as new systems for Aloomba, Edmonton and White Rock and all places in between. I well remember the crowd of locals in Norman St, Gordonvale, in 1952 when they celebrated the official opening of their new supply.

Mayor Bill Fulton declared in 1954 that Behana Creek would ensure no further water restrictions would be necessary in Cairns, but within two years he had to withdraw his statement and restrictions were enforced again. Augmentation of Behana Creek in 1963-64 provided a better supply, but by the early 1970s the water board was looking to Copperlode as the next step to ensure the city's water supply beyond 2000.

I was in on the ground floor, so to speak, of planning for Copperlode Dam in as much as I was in one of the early parties to inspect the site. One thing I clearly remember about those early days was a prediction from the mayor, Dave de Jarlais, that Copperlode Dam would not only guarantee a reliable water supply for Cairns for years to come but would became one of the district's most prized recreation areas. It was said at the time that Copperlode would cope with any increased demand for water in Cairns until 2000, but I have

always thought that no one could have had the foresight to predict the great increase in population and visitor numbers which followed the opening of Cairns International Airport in 1984 and a water supply to meet that need. However, former city engineer Graeme Haussmann once told me he was adamant Copperlode Dam would be adequate for our needs until 2010-15, even if an inflated fabric dam had to be added to the spillway to increase storage capacity, which he said was a quite feasible engineering procedure.

Speculation at the time of the inspection in the early 1970s included that Copperlode may have been named for a local tribe of Aborigines whose name sounded like Copperlode, while others believed it was named by early mineral prospectors who believed they saw traces of copper in the rocks in the area. Copperlode Dam was officially opened on March 25, 1976 by the president of the Cairns Mulgrave Water Supply Board, John Lazarus, a city alderman who for many years owned a general grocery store in Spence St, Bungalow with his brother Ernie.

Cairns, like many other Australian cities, now finds itself looking at inadequate water supplies in the immediate future. But local authorities could hardly be blamed for the situation as it has been well documented that plans were well in hand in the late 1980s for a new dam at Flaggy Creek, which joins the Barron River upstream from Kuranda, with a treatment plant at Lake Placid. World Heritage declaration of the Wet Tropics in 1988 brought with it many advantages, but the abandonment of the Flaggy Creek scheme, as well as another at Tully-Millstream, was not one of them.

In the late 1970s, many issues emerged which would encourage the involvement of activists and exercise the minds of Cairns people for years to come. They included care for the environment, Aboriginal and Islander rights, women's equality, animal welfare and road safety.

Mick Miller, Joe McGinness and Rose Colless were among the pioneers of Aboriginal and Islander activism whom I knew at this time. I first met Mick Miller when he was a school teacher and a rugby league fullback of no mean talent with the Kangaroos club in Cairns. Mick's political career started in the mid-1960s when he joined the local Aboriginal Advancement League and later the Federal Council for the Advancement of Aboriginal and Torres Strait Islanders (FCAATSI). He helped form the influential and original North Queensland Land Council (NQLC) in the early 1970s. Politicians on both sides often sought his advice on policy matters. In early 1981, Mick was a founding member of the Wu Chopperen Medical Service in Cairns. He also became commissioner with the Aboriginal Development Commission (ADC) and later deputy chair. He then espoused a belief being articulated in modern Australia by Noel Pearson that economic development was the key to getting Aboriginal people off welfare and government dependence. In 1985, the government appointed him to head up a review into

employment, education and training. The resultant "Miller Report" became the authority on conduct of federal training and employment programs for many years and was a blueprint on how government programs would be delivered. Mick Miller's untimely death on April 5, 1998 aged only 61 cost the Aboriginal people and this community a respected and vigorous campaigner for social justice.

Joe McGinness was one of the best-loved and respected leaders of the Aboriginal community. I was one of dozens of people who regarded as a friend this quiet, unassuming man whose remarkable achievements involved many of the defining battles for indigenous rights in the Northern Territory, Queensland and nationally. Among many positions, Joe was president of the Federal Council for Aboriginal Advancement for all but one of the years between 1961 and 1978. He counted among his good friends the noted

Joe McGinness, pictured standing at right at Queensland University in 1967, was one of the most active and best loved leaders of the Aboriginal community. Widely known and loved throughout the northern parts of Australia as "Uncle Joe", he died in Cairns on July 11, 2003, aged 89.

Right: Joan Trewern until her death in 2005 was one of the region's foremost activists for women's rights and a prolific contributor to *The Cairns Post* letters section.

Far right: Cairns city councillor and former deputy mayor Margaret Gill was one of the founders of the Cairns Businesswomen's Club in the early 1980s. The club initially had about 100 members but its membership has grown to more than 370 today.

authors Frank Hardy and Xavier Herbert. He credited Herbert with motivating him and others into becoming more active on Aboriginal rights. Joe was a member of the National Aboriginal Consultative Council, the first Federal Government body of indigenous advisers. He was active in establishing Aboriginal hostels in Cairns through the 1970s and 1980s. He was widely known and loved across northern Australia as "Uncle Joe" and was awarded an Order of Australia in recognition of his work for indigenous Australians. Joe died in Cairns on July 11, 2003, aged 89.

Rose Colless was awarded an OAM in 1984 for outstanding personal endeavour in the cause of human rights for the Aboriginal and Torres Strait Islander people in Far North Queensland. She worked intensively in drug and alcohol rehabilitation and for 11 years was manager of the Aborigines and Islander Alcohol Relief Service Limited in Cairns, and ran a meal service in the parks of Cairns, catering for homeless Aborigines.

Joan Trewern, who died in 2005 aged 81, was for 30 years the region's foremost activist on women's issues. Joan, a former Melbourne high school teacher, Jean Bleyerveld, Pat

O'Hara and Ruth Thomas founded the city's first shelter for victims of domestic violence in the late 1970s. Joan joined the Cairns branch of the Women's Electoral Lobby (WEL) soon after it was set up in 1976, became its secretary and produced its monthly newsletter. She was the visible presence of the organisation in this region for the rest of her life. She was a regular correspondent to *The Cairns Post's* letters pages and often dropped her contributions into my office. She was never backward in ticking me off when she thought the newspaper erred in use of gender terminology or what she believed was inadequate coverage of women's sport and other issues.

No woman had sat on a local council until Shirley Harwood of Babinda was elected to the Mulgrave Shire Council in 1973. She retained her seat for 12 years. Jess Mitchell was the first woman to gain a place on the Cairns City Council. She was appointed to fill a casual vacancy caused by the death in office of George Petersen in 1966. But Mrs Mitchell failed to hold her seat in the 1967 election and had been unsuccessful when she was a candidate in the 1964 polls. Joan Wright, one of the city's foremost advocates for environmental and women's issues, filled a casual vacancy on the Cairns City Council in 1972. Wright and Helen Hogan became the first women to be voted on to the council when they contested the 1976 election for the Civic Team. More women made their way on to both councils in the years ahead and in the March 2000 election, no fewer than 16 offered themselves to the voters for the Cairns City Council.

The Cairns Business Women's Club has played a major role in lifting the profile of women in Cairns over the past 25 years. As editor of *The Cairns Post*, I was privy to their plans to form the club in the early 1980s when Margaret Gill and Sue Finch were at the forefront of the movement. I encouraged their activities and in fact once suggested they could quickly raise the profile of women in business if they put together a full team of their members to contest the Cairns City Council election. But they politely declined to act on my suggestion. Their foundation office-bearers were Margaret Gill as president; secretary Yvonne Morgan, who was the first female manager of a Queensland shopping centre; and treasurer the late Robyn Rumble, a partner in the first Ray White franchise in Cairns.

Publicity officer was Sue Finch, proprietor of Gumtree Corner at North Cairns, and a pioneer of the T-shirt industry in Australia. Robyn Stewart of Figures won the first Business Woman of the Year, which I helped to judge. Margaret Gill reminded me recently that in the early 1980s a lot of Cairns businesses were family owned and it was difficult for the wife to have the time off for night functions, so a lunchtime business meeting was therefore most successful.

The club initially had more than 100 members and for a while it was difficult to find venues large enough to cater for the numbers. The club now has some 370 members and it was estimated in recent years that they contributed about $180 million to the region's economy.

People and authorities are more conscious of animal welfare these days, but former Kuranda resident Marjorie Spear made it her personal battle in the 1970s when she helped to set up a refuge for unwanted pets. Mrs Spear, who had moved here from New Zealand, was horrified at the state

of accommodation for stray dogs at Stratford and advertised in *The Cairns Post* for those interested in improving the conditions. She was joined by Dorothy and Charles Brown and their daughter Linda and they set about building a respectable refuge for dogs and cats. Cairns City Council gave them the land and house. Other volunteers joined. They collected money and put up kennels and a cattery. Mrs Spear convinced *The Cairns Post* and its sister weekly paper Cairnsweek to run a regular feature "Dog (and Cat) of the Week" to find homes for their stray animals. "It was a long, hard struggle," Mrs Spear once told me of those early times. Plaques were erected at the refuge in December 2001, as a lasting tribute to the pioneering work of Mrs Spear and Mrs Brown who had taken on the job of refuge manager.

Road safety became an important issue in the 1970s. Community awareness was raised largely through the efforts of Ross Wintour, who for many years was chairman of the Cairns branch of the Road Safety Council. Ross peppered *The Cairns Post* and other media outlets with press releases on the need for courtesy and attention to road rules to prevent the increasing incidence of vehicle accidents.

He was also a strong advocate for governments to provide a better roads system for Far North Queensland. Gordon Trinca, a Melbourne surgeon and road trauma expert who had a second home at Port Douglas, was also very active on this issue in the 1970s. Police around this time were also becoming more vigilant of motorists driving while under the influence of alcohol. I remember how the late Bill Jenkins, a sergeant of police stationed at Cairns, ran something of a personal crusade against drink-drivers.

Bill often placed himself at strategic positions near hotels to snare offenders. In those days before random breath testing methods were introduced, suspect motorists were made to undertake basic roadside sobriety tests like touching the point of their nose with their forefinger which could lead to their arrest. *The Cairns Post* in the 1970s published details of all court cases and it was something of a regular event for readers to scan Tuesday's paper to see the names of the

Protesters gather at Mt Windsor Tableland on the western side of Daintree in November 1981 in Far North Queensland's first major protest against logging of rainforests.

motorists who had been caught for drink driving.

Concern for the environment in the Cairns district will always be associated with the hippie culture in the early 1970s when young people sought an alternate lifestyle. Many settled in a commune at Kuranda. The first protesters' blockade against logging of rainforests in Queensland was held at the Mt Windsor Tableland, west of the Daintree during October 1981. *The Cairns Post* provided extensive coverage although it did not become a national news item. But it was regarded as the event which led to the Hawke Labor government moving towards World Heritage listing of rainforests in 1988.

These early protests were often summarily dismissed by the wider community as the work of ratbags, and the alternate lifestyle protesters were subjected to taunts of "hippie dole bludgers", "the great unwashed" and "rent a crowd". I recall how the timber industry in particular was dismissive of their objections and seemed to be affronted that *The Cairns Post* covered their protests against logging of old growth forests. I attended a timber industry dinner in Cairns one

night around this time and sat through speaker after speaker ridiculing the efforts of protesters. They also poured scorn on me and the newspaper for giving the protests legitimacy by publicising the activities.

However, the "hippie" protesters no longer became easy targets when academics and local business and professional people began to join their ranks out of concern for other issues besides the forests. They included pollution of rivers and streams, over-development of hillslopes, and potential damage to the Great Barrier Reef from agricultural runoff and exposure to an increasing number of daily visitors.

One of the earlier activists came from a most unlikely sector of the community. He was Wally O'Grady, a farmer from the Gordonvale area. Wally's passion for conservation was instrumental in the World Wildlife Congress being held in Cairns in June 1980 when some 1000 delegates from 25 countries attended. He was the congress chairman. Prime Minister Malcolm Fraser, when opening the congress, recommended that the Great Barrier Reef become a World Heritage site.

The increasing concern for the environment spawned other special interest organisations, including CAFNEC (Cairns and Far North Environment Centre) where I recall Rosemary Hill was one of the most prominent organisers. CAFNEC set up its first office in Andrejic Arcade in Lake St. Another was the Trinity Bay and Inlet Protection Society. It was led for many years by Cairns-born orthopaedic surgeon Mike Mansfield out of his concern about the deteriorating state of the inlet caused by pollutants. The society was directly responsible for changing practices at the city dump at Portsmith when in the mid-1980s it exposed by scientific examination that leachate flowing unchecked from the dump into the estuary was destroying the inlet's fish habitat. The society organised the rally of more than 7000 people on the Esplanade in 1989 to oppose the proposed Trinity Point development of the inlet.

The wider issue of preservation of rainforests became a major national news event late in 1983 when the Douglas Shire Council, with the blessing of the Queensland government, decided to build a 32km road from Cape Tribulation to Bloomfield through a recently declared national park. Images of protesters chained to trees and blocking the path of bulldozers were flashed around Australia and the Daintree soon became a household name associated with the conversation battle against logging of forests. The road was completed in October 1984 and hailed by proponents as a major victory. The conservation movement gained momentum in the years ahead which led to World Heritage listing of rainforests in 1988. It brought to a close the timber industry as Far North Queensland once knew it when even the smallest towns in the district had a sawmill providing employment for their locals. While many in the timber industry blamed the conservation movement and governments for their demise, a different view was held by the late Len Smith, a former Ravenshoe logging contractor and respected member of the industry for 50 years. Smith wrote in his book *The Trees That Fell*: "There is no doubt that man's greed coupled with his lack of understanding of the forest led to the state it was in when Heritage legislation was introduced. To think this vast area was ravaged in less than 100 years shows what lack of understanding of the forests' needs and exploitation can do."

Douglas shire chairman Tony Mijo (left) and member for Barron River and state environment minister Martin Tenni claim victory over conservationists as the Cape Tribulation to Bloomfield road is pushed through on October 7, 1984.

MOMENTS IN TIME

1970 – April 21
Queen visits Cairns briefly on way to Cooktown as part of 200-year Captain Cook Discovery anniversary celebrations.

1971 – September 25
New fire station is officially opened in Gatton St, transferred from Lake St where today's parking station is located.

1971 – October 4
New hospital block is opened at Cairns Base with maternity and surgical sections.

1972 – February 12
Cenotaph is moved from Abbott and Shields street intersection to the Esplanade.

1972 – May 27
First residents enter Farnorha, city's first home for the aged.

1972 – June 6
Koch Memorial is moved from Abbott and Spence streets intersection to Anzac Park.

1972 – October 7
Captain Cook motel in Sheridan St starts advertising.

1972 – November 22
Coles New World supermarket opens in Sheridan St (closing in 1997).

1972 – December 14
Traffic lights used for first time at Abbott/Shields and Lake/Shields intersections.

1972 – December 20
Opening of Odeon in Grafton St, city's first airconditioned theatre.

Traffic lights operated in the CBD of Cairns for the first time on December 14, 1972; in Shields St at the Lake and Abbott streets intersections.

MOMENTS IN TIME

1972 – December 21
First transmission of Channel 10 TV programs from Bellenden Ker.

1973 – September 8
Royal Flying Doctor Base opens in Cairns.

1973 – October 27
Australian Government office building in Shields St opens.

1974 – February 1
HMAS Cairns facility at 16 Grafton St is commissioned.

1974 – May 31
Cairns Civic Centre is opened by PM Gough Whitlam.

1974 – June 29
Night harness racing starts at Cairns Showground.

1974 – December 4
City's first shopping centre opens at Raintrees in Manunda.

1975 – February
Motorcycle shop proprietor Rusty Rees starts Rusty's Markets in Grafton St.

1975 – March 1
Colour TV transmission starts Australia-wide with ABC *Countdown* program.

1975 – October 23
Hawker de Havilland aircraft from Mt Isa crashes in cane paddock at Holloways

Beach during approach to airport in heavy rainstorm, killing all 11 on board.

1976 – February 20
Commonwealth Bank relocates from corner Abbott and Spence streets to Lake St.

1976 – March 25
Copperlode Dam (Lake Morris) with holding capacity of 45,000 megalitres is officially opened.

1976 – October 9
Memorial unveiled on Esplanade near Cairns Base Hospital in memory of 320 airmen who died on Catalina flying boats based at Cairns in World War II.

The HMAS Cairns facility at 16 Grafton St was commissioned on February 1, 1974. It then had only four officers and 30 sailors. In May 1982, its $14 million naval base was officially opened. In recent years, more than 1500 personnel have been based at Cairns to crew and service two hydrographic survey ships, four heavy landing craft, four survey motor launches and six patrol boats.

MOMENTS IN TIME

1976 – October 9
Year-long celebrations of centenary
of Cairns settlement culminates in the
Centenary Cavalcade through city streets.

1976 – December 17
Centenary Lakes opened opposite Botanic
Gardens.

1977 – June 30
School of Arts and library, corner Shields
and Lake streets, closes and hands over
to Cairns City Council.

1977 – December 16
New Barron River bridge at Stratford
opens.

1978 – April 9
Mayor David de Jarlais dies in office.

1978 – August 12
New concrete bridge over Barron River at
Stratford opens.

1979 – February 3
New city library opens at 123 Lake St,
former site of F.R. Ireland motor dealer.

1979 – June 30
Cairns Aerial Ambulance hands over to
Flying Doctor Service after making 6451
trips since established in 1937.

1979 – December 14
First colour telecasts from Channel 9 in
Townsville.

Motorcycle shop proprietor Rusty Rees started his now-famous Rusty's Markets in Grafton St in February 1975.

Prime Minister Gough Whitlam officially opened the Cairns Civic Centre on May 30, 1974 when a huge crowd began flocking to the building more than a hour before the scheduled opening. It was PM Whitlam's first official function after his Labor government had been returned to office.

City Place soon after it was officially opened at corner of Shields and Lake streets on August 18, 1984. Cairns City Council said at the time the creation of "a place for people" was its ambition to provide "a scenic focal point for the public to meet, relax and soak up some of the local Cairns atmosphere". Council as early as 1977 conducted studies with business operators and owners directly affected, but it did not proceed due to lack of support by some businesses. A week-long series of festivities was held to open the City Place, which the council hoped would set a pattern for the type of family entertainment to be held there.

Chapter seven - 1980s

The event which had the greatest single impact on Cairns during my lifetime was the opening of Cairns International Airport on Saturday, March 31, 1984. It changed Cairns almost overnight from a steadily growing city in the tropics to a world-renowned tourist destination. With the benefits it brought, it is almost impossible now to comprehend the level of opposition and anger at the time to the proposition of local ownership of the airport.

The concept was never fully understood by the general public, despite the best efforts of its proponents through the media and so clearly articulated at public meetings. Basically, it meant that ownership would be transferred by the federal government to a local authority with a negotiated sum of money to upgrade all airport facilities to an agreed standard.

The main issue clouding the debate was a claim that the cost of running the airport could become an impost on ratepayers, a claim that never had any basis in fact.

By the early 1970s, the Cairns aerodrome and its facilities had deteriorated to such an extent that only basic maintenance was being carried out. Civic leaders were worried the city's future as a major domestic airport would diminish if a major upgrade was not carried out. The federal government offered local ownership to many cities throughout Australia. Cairns City Council under Mayor Ron Davis tried to enlist the support of other local authorities to form a statutory body to administer the airport under local ownership – first raised as the answer to the airport problems at a meeting of community leaders on January 15, 1979. But only Eacham and Atherton

Cairns International Airport was officially opened on March 31, 1984 when Qantas flight 747B took off with a full payload of 438 passengers for Honolulu.

gave unequivocal support. Even Mulgrave chairman (later mayor) Tom Pyne, who was a member of the seven-person Cairns Airport Development Committee, could not win support from his council.

On February 24, 1981, the Queensland government said it would not agree to formation of a new statutory body to take control of the airport, and on March 31, 1981, the Cairns Harbour Board (later Cairns Port Authority) under chairman Mick Borzi took over negotiations. Borzi answered persistent criticism by the Cairns Airport Action Committee, which vigorously opposed the airport ownership, that the airport would become a burden on ratepayers by explaining this could not be so as the CPA had no charter to charge rates.

Borzi also had to convince airlines to use the airport. Many, particularly Qantas, resisted for some time before finally announcing in September 1983 it would service Cairns from North America and Asia. From late 1983 into early 1984, Borzi and groups of Cairns businessmen involved in the hospitality industry, including Gordon McKauge, Ray Rogers, Graham Gordon, Charles Woodward, Peter Miller, Paul Kamsler junior, Denis Ferguson and Peter Cryan, made several trips to overseas countries, notably New Zealand, North America, Asia, Europe and the UK, to sell Cairns as a tourist destination.

The official opening of Cairns International Airport was a gala occasion which I was fortunate to have attended with my wife Hilary. A huge crowd attended, estimated at more than 10,000 and even up to 16,000. Many stayed on to cheer and clap the arrival at 8.45pm of Qantas QF25 from the south, en route to Honolulu. It left Cairns at 10.08pm with 438 passengers, about half boarding at Cairns. Qantas had announced the day before that 6000 Americans had already booked flights to visit Australia through Cairns. More than 1000 Cairns people early on the morning of April 3, 1984 welcomed the first Qantas flight from North America and Honolulu, and 258 passengers disembarked in Cairns. It was the trickle of visitors that would become a flood.

Even then, it was inconceivable that within a decade, one million international visitors would be arriving annually or that Cairns would one day become second only to Sydney among Australia's busiest airports. But few of the opponents to local ownership were prepared to admit they were wrong, and many later jumped on the bandwagon of success to claim a share of the credit for taking over the airport. The prevailing attitude was best summed up by David Jull, the long serving federal member of Fadden, who was deputy general manager of the Queensland Tourist and Travel Corporation in 1983-84. Jull wrote in April 1994: "While many would bask in the Cairns glory (now), there was opposition to the whole project from early in the piece. This objection came not only from some sections of the Cairns community, but from outside the city as well. The Australian airlines were never overly enthusiastic about what was planned. Regional areas, jealous of what was being done, white-anted the project as best they could. Many in the press were sceptical."

Mick Borzi's dynamic leadership in the development of Cairns International Airport was officially recognised when he was nominated as one of six finalists for 1984 Queenslander of the Year. Four others were Queensland Ballet Company soloist Rosetta Cook, Brisbane pediatric surgeon Fred Leditschke, Brisbane restaurateur and leader of the Italian community Gino Merlo, and Brisbane theatrical pioneer Rhoda Felgate. As I said in Mick Borzi's official biography that I authored, it says something of Queensland's values when the winner in such an outstanding field of achievers was Ron Grant, whose main claim to fame was being the first man to run around Australia.

A friend once remarked to me that the 1980s should be remembered as "The Exciting Eighties" with so much happening in the city. The opening of Cairns International Airport heralded construction of several major developments in the CBD, including the Hilton Hotel (1986), Parkroyal (later Cairns International, 1988), and the Pier Marketplace (1989).

But even before the opening of the new airport, Cairns's

skyline into the 1980s had begun to change gradually with the emergence of the city's first high-rise buildings. The first in February 1981 was the seven-storey Tuna Towers, corner Abbott and Minnie streets and the Esplanade, and later that year the equally lofty Lyons Vacation Inn, corner Esplanade and Aplin streets. The Aquarius apartments in July 1982 and Pacific International in February 1983 followed soon after. Until then, the city's tallest buildings would have been three storeys and included the Australian Hotel at 19 Abbott St built in 1926, and Bolands in Spence St in 1912-13. Plans for the Lyons Vacation Inn in particular brought on a wave of hysteria among locals fearful that the council decision to allow high-rise buildings signalled the start of Cairns being converted to "another Gold Coast".

However, T.B. O'Meara, the city's leading building contractor, had no such fears. "I have always maintained that Cairns will never become a city of skyscrapers," he said in August 1947. O'Meara, who had his offices and factory at 77 Spence St, was responsible for some of the district's major building projects, including Mt St Bernard's convent and school at Herberton and major renovations to *The Cairns Post* in 1924 and the Commonwealth Bank in Abbott St. Commenting on plans for multi-storey additions to Cairns Base Hospital, O'Meara said he would be "quite prepared to build to five or six storeys in Cairns".

Cairns had its first brush with high-rise buildings late in 1956 when the Cairns-based Queensland construction firm, T.J. Watkins Pty Ltd, began work on the new nurses' quarters at Cairns Base Hospital. *The Cairns Post* reported on October 19, 1956 that at a height of 80feet (24.3m), the five-storey structure would be the tallest building in Cairns when completed after a two-year project. Some 30 years later, Cairns residents did not relish the prospect of further high-rise buildings being approved by their Cairns City Council. In the early 1980s, stories about high-rise building applications, council's attempts to restrict

Work is well under way in 1985 on the new Cairns Hilton, dwarfing the old Cairns Yacht Club. The Hilton was built on the site of the old Cairns swimming baths.

An aerial shot in 1934 of the Strand Hotel on the corner of the Esplanade and Spence St where the Pacific International opened on February 26, 1983, as the city's first in a wave of first class hotels of the 1980s-90s.

Reclamation works under way on the Cairns Esplanade in 1987 for a site on which the Pier Marketplace was constructed.

building heights and public concern filled the columns of *The Cairns Post*.

Cairns City Council in the late 1970s had placed a moratorium on high-rise approvals. Its policy was that consent would not be given to any future high-rise buildings unless they had special features to merit exclusion. Features would have to include exceptional architectural merit; amalgamation of several allotments into one large lot to achieve a more desirable development; landscaped areas well in excess of bylaw requirements; preservation of buildings of historical interest; other features which would make the development a desirable addition to the city; provision of car parking in excess of bylaws. But by April 1981, *The Cairns Post* reported the council had approved 17 high-rise buildings in the area bounded by Wharf to Lily streets and from McLeod St to the Esplanade.

Sally Robertson of Machans Beach put forward a view shared by many locals when she objected in a letter to the paper on August 25, 1981 to allowing high-rise on the Esplanade. "I am wondering if our responsible aldermen realise the discomfort they are inflicting on the majority of Cairns folk by allowing high-rise buildings on the Esplanade," she wrote. "The effect will be like constructing a large wind barrier to stop the sea breeze getting to the inner suburbs and will greatly increase the humidity. Isn't that unnecessary suffering? These high-rise buildings could easily be constructed further back into the mountains where they would not block either the view or the wind and would create a far more attractive picture to Cairns on the whole."

Sue Harris, secretary of the Cairns branch of the National Trust, complained in an article in the *Post* on October 3, 1981 about approval of high-rise buildings along the "Barbary Coast" (lower Abbott-Wharf streets) area. Mrs Harris said one of the main problems was that developers were using Melbourne architects who would not even have seen the site. She said the Wharf St area, with its distinctive "verandahed" hotels, could be developed similar to The Rocks, a historical area in Sydney.

Built in 1905, the Australian Hotel at 19 Abbott St was probably the first building in Cairns higher than two levels. The hotel was demolished in 1987 to make way for the Parkroyal (later Cairns International).

Two old city hotels, the Australian and Criterion, were demolished in 1987 to make way for Cairns's tallest building, the 16-storey Parkroyal Hotel (later Cairns International) which opened in 1988. The Barrier Reef Hotel remained the only one of six pubs that once lined the lower Abbott and Wharf streets area that was known as the Barbary Coast in the days when about 1000 men were employed as labourers on city wharves.

Michael Bryan, a frequent critic of council decision-making on building approvals, wrote to the paper on October 8, 1981 stating: "It is depressing that few local decision-makers seem to be aware of the threat to community identity posed by the power of capital controlled from thousands of kilometres away. Alien values and lifestyles are imposed without the humanising interaction probable when newcomers bringing capital make their home here. Residents who used to have power of decision over their lives are diminished. Businesses which are independent become servants of the agents of the new rulers. If everyone to whom Cairns means more than money does not speak out soon only a busy but pointless concrete shell will remain."

I remember when motels, introduced into Australia from the United States in the 1950s as a new style of accommodation for the travelling public, started to gain in popularity in Cairns. Our first motels were the Cairns Coral at 162 Grafton St, extending through to Lake St, and the Beltana at 380-384 Mulgrave Rd. When *The Cairns Post* published a story on December 30, 1959 on the impending opening of the Cairns Coral, it referred to it as the city's second motel. The article did not name the first, but I had always thought the Coral was the first. The *Post* article said Queensland at the time had only 13 motels and Australia fewer than 80 in total, most of them (48) in NSW. The £40,000 (about $1 million today) 12-unit Coral, owned by local company Walker Estates

Cairns author Xavier Herbert died at Alice Springs on November 10, 1984, aged 83. He lived in Cairns in a cottage at Redlynch from 1946 where he wrote his epic novel, *Poor Fellow My Country*. It won the 1974 Miles Franklin award. After his wife Sadie died in 1979, Herbert left Cairns in January 1984 to move to Alice Springs.

Pty Ltd and built by R.C. Harder, provided rooms at £2 a night (about $50 today). Tom Walker, a director of Walker Estates, told *The Cairns Post* the company had intended building flats on the property but he had been impressed by the new motels he had seen in NSW during a motoring holiday with his wife, and thought they would build a motel in Cairns instead. The Cairns Coral proudly boasted that units were airconditioned, with private showers and toilets, inner spring beds, parking for vehicles outside each suite, and an electric jug with tea and sugar in each unit. Laundry facilities were provided and breakfast and dinner were available in a modern restaurant.

The Beltana, which was trading by early 1962, was also airconditioned with similar features to the Cairns Coral. Other early Cairns motels in later years were the Lyons in Abbott St and the Siesta and Pengana (both on the Esplanade). The *Post* report quoted an industry spokesman as stating Queensland's new motels were catering for about 50,000 Victorian motorists travelling north each year and some 80,000 from NSW.

The new Cairns International Airport provided the impetus for a surge in visitors to this city. But few locals appreciate that the tourist industry dates back almost to the time of the city's settlement. New hotels built in the 1890s and 1900s were aimed at capturing the holiday market. They included Hides and McColl's that opened in 1890 and the Strand in 1901. Southerners loved Kuranda as a honeymoon destination. Photos of the time depict visitors enjoying a game of croquet on the lawn of the Kuranda Hotel and boating on the Barron River below the hotel.

The Queensland Government Tourist Bureau and other state government agencies were actively promoting tourism 100 years ago. An entry in the 1910 Queensland Railways handbook on Cairns and district recommended a rail trip from Brisbane to Gladstone, then by steamer through the Whitsunday Islands to Cairns, as an ideal holiday tour.

The tourism boom and construction of new hotels in Cairns in the 1980s received a major setback from the Australia-wide pilots' strike from August 18, 1989 to January 1990. It was one of the most expensive and dramatic industrial disputes in

Australia's history, and cost an estimated $500 million to the national economy and about $60 million to the Cairns region. Many businesses took years to recover, but the strike sent others to the wall. Hotels and restaurants tried to attract more trade from local residents by offering special rates for rooms and meals.

Cairns author Xavier Herbert died at Alice Springs on November 10, 1984, aged 83. It was a personal loss for me. We became good friends in the early 1970s, just before publication of his epic novel, *Poor Fellow My Country*. At 1463 pages and 850,000 words, it is one of the longest novels ever published in English. It won the 1974 Miles Franklin award. Herbert wrote the novel in a shed at the rear of the cottage next door to the Redlynch pub where he had moved in 1946 with his wife Sadie until she died in 1979.

Herbert turned his back on Cairns when he left on January 15, 1984 to live in Alice Springs. Some writers said he had resolved to go back to his roots to die. Not so. First, the "dead heart" was not his roots. He spent his early life in Geraldton on the coast of Western Australia. I believe it was simply that he greatly missed Sadie and could not continue to live in the cottage with so many memories of the life they shared there for so many years. But rather than accepting his pending demise, he in fact told me he had intended writing another great novel. We spoke on the phone almost every day and I used to visit him once a week at his Redlynch home. He cooked me lunch and we yarned for a couple of hours.

During one of these sessions, he spoke about the new novel he would be writing when he settled in Alice Springs. It was to be about the union movement, titled *Billy Goat Hill*. He surprised me by asking for my help: "When I've written the first draft, man, I'll get you to come out and read it," he said. "I don't want to make a fool of myself."

But I did not speak to Herbert again after he left Cairns in his four-wheel drive towing a special trailer he had outfitted for that great journey out of his former life to a new one in Alice Springs. My wife Hilary and I were staying in a Sydney hotel after a newspaper conference when *The Cairns Post* rang me around mid-evening on that Sunday in November 1984 to say that Xavier had died that day. However, I had received a long letter that he wrote to me from Hughenden, dated February 17, 1984. Parts of the letter give a clue as to his state of mind. He apologised for not seeing me on the day that he had left Cairns, saying, "I was wishing to save my soul." Of his journey at times through heavy rain, he said, "But it was great fun because at last I was free, free, free (of what?)." And then: "I still can't escape fame. It is amazing that even in remote places, people know me: in post offices, stores, pubs. But I soon escape from them. God save me from my fame, too, I can take care of my infamy." His letter ended: "Perhaps we shall never meet again. If so, I must say that I shall be eternally grateful for your warm and intelligent friendship. Most sincerely yours, Xavier."

I was proud of the genuine friendship we shared. But Xavier Herbert was regarded by many locals as an eccentric at a time when the Cairns community generally did not appreciate the wealth of artistic talent that we had in this district. Other more widely acclaimed artists who began to gain local recognition around this time included novelist Thea Astley, painter Ray Crooke, Ansett pilot, author and painter Percy Trezise, and Aboriginal artists Thancoupie and Dick Roughsey.

Thea Astley and her husband Jack Gregson moved in 1980 to live at Kuranda and write full-time after teaching at several schools in Sydney. Tropical North Queensland was often the setting for her books because she delighted in our smaller communities. She once said about her life in Kuranda: "It was the smallness of the place and the scenery that blew my mind, and it was full of screwballs." She said the demise of that world was what really killed her desire to write: "The last time I saw Cairns and Kuranda they'd become tourist destinations full of plastic chairs and buses."

Ms Astley left Kuranda in the late 1980s for Nowra on the NSW south coast and then to Byron Bay where she died in 2004. Her novels won four Miles Franklin awards and

Thea Astley, one of Australia's most prolific novelists, once lived at Kuranda where she wrote some of her books, four of which won Miles Franklin awards. Ms Astley died in Byron Bay in 2004.

in 1989 she won the Patrick White Award for services to Australian literature. She was awarded an honorary doctorate by the University of Queensland in 1989.

Ray Crooke was born in Victoria in 1922, but he has lived for much of his adult life in the Cairns district. Crooke first encountered the northern landscape as a young man when he enlisted in the army and travelled from Western Australia to Townsville, through Cape York Peninsula and the Atherton Tableland to Chillagoe and to Thursday Island, where he worked as a map-maker.

These initial observations of vegetation, climate, hue and light underpinned his techniques as a landscape painter, and paved a way for many paintings in the 1960-70s. His powerful imagery and vibrant colours have made Crooke one of Australia's most highly regarded artists. His paintings have been widely shown at the Australian Galleries, Melbourne, also in Sydney, Brisbane, Perth, Adelaide and also in London at the Australian Art Exhibition, Tate Gallery, 1963, and a one-man show at Leicester Galleries in 1974. His murals grace Australia House in London and his painting, The Offering 1971, is in the Vatican Museum collection. In 1969, Crooke won the Archibald Prize of the Art Gallery of NSW

for his portrait of George Johnston, author of the Australian classic My Brother Jack.

Percy Trezise, a great friend of Xavier Herbert, was one of this city's most remarkable citizens and a larger than life character whom I knew well. Author, painter, pilot and rock art historian, Percy was instrumental in allowing precious Aboriginal images to be seen by contemporary eyes.

Percy, who died in Cairns on May 10, 2003, aged 82, also was a dedicated conservationist. In the mid-1970s, when the Fraser federal government had granted woodchip export licences, he led the fight to stop woodchipping in North Queensland rainforests. He painted many landscapes, wrote dozens of children's books, found the great cave art repositories of Cape York and encouraged North Queensland Aboriginal artists and writers. During the 1960s, his job as an Ansett pilot allowed him to fly regularly over the sites of the Quinkan rock art. He explored by air and foot areas likely to contain Aboriginal rock art.

He discovered more than 1000 galleries of rock art in the Cape York area, some more than 20,000 years old. Travelling on a Churchill Fellowship in 1972 to look at major rock art overseas, he concluded that Cape York offered probably the largest body of rock art in the world. He spent years making an extensive record of paintings and drawings of the landscapes of Cape York Peninsula, many of which he donated to James Cook University. He "discovered" the Quinkans in 1959 and spent the next 30 years locating and photographing the sites. To protect this extensive body of rock art, he lobbied to have the Laura district declared a reserve, which was achieved in 1975. He wrote several books on Aboriginal art and culture, including *Quinkan Country* and *Last Days of Wilderness*, and many children's books with a conservation theme.

Percy was instrumental in encouraging many Aboriginal artists, painters and potters, including Thancoupie, the great potter from Weipa, and author Dick Roughsey, whose Aboriginal name was Goobalathaldin, from Mornington Island. In a traditional ceremony, Percy became Dick Roughsey's brother and was given the Aboriginal name of Warrenby. Dick came from Mornington Island. He first came to the world's attention when he published a number of children's books with Percy Tresize. Their books were about dreamtime stories, one of which, *The Rainbow Serpent*, had special meaning to Dick Roughsey. Legend has it that when

the Rainbow Serpent had finished creating the land, seas and mountains, it finished its journey at Mornington Island. Dick Roughsey died in 1985.

Thancoupie was born Gloria Fletcher in 1937 at Napranum on Cape York Peninsula. She attended the local school before being sent to Brisbane to train as a preschool teacher. Upon her return to Napranum, she established a preschool but was unhappy with the situation and resigned.

Thancoupie began writing down and illustrating (with paintings on bark) stories her grandmother had taught her, and had a number of exhibitions of her work. Her application to study at a Sydney art school was rejected because she lacked formal qualifications, but she came across a pottery school which accepted her as a student. Thancoupie then went to America and Mexico and worked with indigenous potters.

This helped her develop her own style, and she has since been creating pots and tile murals at her studio in Cairns where she moved in 1976. She won the 2006 Australia Council for the Arts' visual arts emeritus award which included a $40,000 prize. Locals who bought Thancoupie's early paintings and pottery for a few dollars in the 1970s now have valuable works of art in their possession.

Percy Trezise was one of Cairns's most remarkable citizens and a larger than life character. Author, painter, pilot and rock art historian, Percy was instrumental in allowing precious Aboriginal images to be seen by contemporary eyes. Percy, who died in Cairns in May 2003, aged 82, was also a dedicated conservationist.

The decade of the 1980s ended with the two worst tragedies affecting Cairns people during my lifetime. The Gillies Highway bus crash on February 4, 1987 was the most gut-wrenching news story I have been involved with. That terrible loss of young lives was the only time in my newspaper career I have been reduced to tears. Students from Cairns State High School's Year 12 were returning from a leadership camp at Tinaroo when at about 1pm the second of three buses failed to take a bend and toppled over the side. Seven students died at the scene, and another died in Gordonvale Hospital from injuries. They were Amanda Garrone, 16, Monique Perrem, 16, Erica Strooper, 16, Elizabeth Zeimer, 17, Judith Frerichs, 17, Mark Fisher, 16, Lee-Ann Willis, 16, and Jody Keen, 16. Two teachers and a further 33 students were injured, 12 seriously. Two inquests were held and one found that the bus's brakes were faulty and absolved the bus driver from any blame for the crash.

Journalists try to hold themselves aloof from terrible events they have to report, but we at *The Cairns Post* shared the anguish of anxious parents of the students. One of our own, the late Brian Gunn, learned that his daughter Lisa was on one of the buses. As many parents did that day, Brian and wife Val went through many anxious moments before they found that Lisa had been on the bus following the one that had crashed. St Monica's Cathedral was packed with mourners a week later when a memorial service was held for the eight students who died. Queensland Premier Sir Joh Bjelke-Petersen addressed the congregation.

The evening of May 11, 1990 marked one of the worst nightmares I have ever been involved with. At around 5.40pm that Friday, a Cessna 500 VH-ANQ executive jet plunged at full speed into the eastern slopes of Mt Emerald, 15km south of Mareeba. All 11 on board were killed including Cairns mayor Keith Goodwin and his deputy Rose Blank. Others who died were Atherton councillor Ivan Wilkinson, Eacham councillors Joe Newman and Hec Wallace, Herberton councillors Harry Rankine, Graham Luxton and Elwyn Phillips, Douglas councillor Bruno Reidweg, Sister Nadia

Students unveil a memorial plaque at Cairns State High School on February 5, 1988, one year after eight Grade 12 students were killed in a bus crash on the Gillies Highway.

Giovanna del Popolo of Cairns, and pilot Stan Lindgren of Cairns. The councillors had been attending a local government conference at Airlie Beach and were making their way to Cairns via Mareeba. They were due to land at Mareeba airport at 6.30pm. Bad weather, pilot error and bad luck were all blamed for the flight never completing its approach. Wreckage was scattered across 600m of mountain ridge. Atherton mayor Jim Chapman and Mulgrave mayor Tom Pyne were supposed to be on board. Sister del Popolo took Cr Chapman's seat after he cancelled his booking a couple of days before to attend a meeting in Brisbane.

A Bureau of Air Safety investigation was inconclusive and the cause remained undetermined. Investigators said the plane was unlikely to have been affected by weather conditions and there was no suggestion the pilot suffered any sudden illness. In 1991, Coroner Hamilton Spicer said the cause of the accident remained undetermined but relatives of those who died believed pilot error was at fault. "The pilot has descended 6400 feet to the crash site, some 5.5km off the reported track having been ordered to maintain 10,000 feet," Mr Spicer said in his findings.

Keith Goodwin, former head of TAFE in Cairns, in March 1988 had led the new Alliance Team to office in the Cairns City Council elections, ousting the Ron Davis Civic group in a landslide victory to win seven of the other eight seats. Goodwin won the day with his vision of preserving a quality of life for residents against the accelerated development taking place, and care for the environment. He coined the slogan, "Cairns. Where people make the difference." Goodwin will best be remembered for helping to scuttle the $500 million Trinity Point proposal to develop 81ha of Trinity Inlet, which would have resulted in the most grotesque distortion of this city's landscape that anyone could imagine. It would have included a long spit of land linked to an "island" in the middle of the inlet. About 25,000 people signed a petition against it and more than 7000 attended a rally on the Esplanade one Sunday in October 1989 when Goodwin waded out in the muddy foreshore to plant a flag

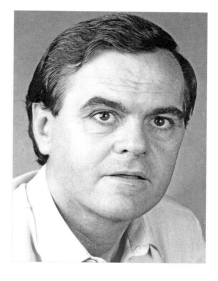

Keith Goodwin, the former mayor of Cairns who was killed in an aircraft crash at Mt Emerald, near Tolga, on May 11, 1990. Ald Goodwin led the new Alliance Team to a stunning election victory over Ron Davis's Civic Team in March 1988. He was elected on a platform of care for the environment and to provide a better lifestyle for the residents of Cairns.

and symbolically reclaim the foreshore for the people of Cairns. Soon after, National Party Premier Russell Cooper announced the state government was dropping its support.

Reporting such a dramatic and tragic event as the plane crash would have been stressful enough for an editor and his staff, but about four hours before the aircraft smashed into Mt Emerald every journalist and photographer employed at *The Cairns Post* had walked off the job in support of their union's pay claim. It was a time when no journalist dared to challenge the mantra of union solidarity, regardless of the importance of reporting even a major event like the Mt Emerald crash. They left the huge Saturday edition barely half-done. I was alone to complete the task, designing pages, placing stories and photos, and writing headlines.

Only the newspaper's accountant John Letson offered help. Throughout the night, Letson answered phones, acted as a gofer and provided moral support. He gave me news of the crash around 8.30pm. I telephoned Mulgrave Shire mayor Tom Pyne close to midnight to ask what he knew. With no names released officially or on news services, I settled into writing the front-page story after 1.30am, already 90 minutes past deadline. Despite the difficulties, that important edition of the paper was published and delivered by early morning.

MOMENTS IN TIME

1980 – June 21
Cairns Historical Society museum opens in School of Arts building.

1980 – November 28
The Bookshelf opens in Grafton St selling secondhand books to support Cairns Women's Shelter crisis accommodation.

1980 – October 2
$1 million water slide and spa pool opens in Lake St.

1980 – May 21
Imperial Hotel, corner Abbott and Shields streets, ceases trading.

1980 – November 5
Earlville Shoppingtown (now Stockland Earlville) opens.

1980 – November 19
Kamerunga Bridge opens to traffic.

1981 – February 20
Era of high-rise development starts with seven-storey Tuna Towers apartments, followed on October 2 by Lyons Vacation Inn.

1981 – June 21
New Calvary Hospital officially opens.

1981 – November 1
Cairns Harbour Board assumes responsibility for local ownership of Cairns airport and changes its name to Cairns Port Authority.

1981 – November 24
Old Cairns Harbour Board dredge Trinity Bay towed out to sea and sunk by RAAF bombers near Euston Reef.

1982 – March 20
New municipal carpark in Lake St opens.

1982 – May 28
New $8.8 million HMAS Cairns base in Draper St officially opens.

1982 – July 17
Aquarius, city's tallest building at 16 storeys, opens on Esplanade.

1983 – January 17
Westcourt Plaza opens.

1983 – February 26
Pacific International Hotel opens on

Spence St site of old Strand Hotel.

1983 – June
Cairns Little Theatre's Rondo opens in Greenslopes St.

1984 – March 18
Botanic Gardens officially named Flecker Memorial Gardens.

1984 – March 31
Official opening of Cairns International Airport and first Qantas flight to Honolulu.

1984 – August 18
City Place officially opens at corner of Shields and Lake streets.

1984 – November 10
Death of Cairns author Xavier Herbert whose epic novel *Poor Fellow My Country* published in 1975 won the Miles Franklin Award.

1985 – October 7
First Japan Air Lines charter flight of tourists arrives.

1986 – February 2
Cyclone Winifred hits wide area of district causing most damage in Innisfail area.

Damage was strewn over a wide area of Bunda and Spence streets after an explosion at the Cairns Gas Corporation works at 3pm on August 15, 1987. One man died and 23 were injured. Estimated damage was $7 million when a gas leak from a split hose exploded. Reverberations from the blast were felt many kilometres away and buildings in Abbott St shook.

MOMENTS IN TIME

1986 – March 18
Smithfield Shopping Centre opens.

1986 – July 1
The Cairns Post newspaper changes from broadsheet format to tabloid.

1987 – February 4
Eight Cairns State High students killed when bus crashes off Gillies Highway.

1987 – August 17
One man dies and 23 others injured in Bunda St gas explosion.

1987 – December
Barlow Park opens with seating for 400.

1988 – February 27
Mangrove boardwalk opens off main Cairns airport road.

1988 – July 6
16-storey Parkroyal Hotel (later Cairns International) opens in as city's tallest building in same Abbott St precinct of city's first buildings in 1880s.

1989
Johno's Blues Bar (closed in June 2007) opens in Sheridan St.

1989 – August
Pilots' strike begins Australia-wide, causing massive damage to Far North Queensland's tourism industry.

1989 – October 1
7000 crowd at Esplanade rally to protest at Trinity Point development.

1989 – November 28
Pier Marketplace opens on reclaimed Esplanade area.

Stranded holidaymakers and other passengers were transported out of Cairns in an RAAF Hercules during the Australia-wide pilots' strike which started in August 1989 and ended in January 1990. It caused massive damage to the Cairns district's tourism industry.

The new Cairns City Council elected in March 1995 after amalgamation with Mulgrave Shire: (front from left) Bob Burgess, Bishop James Foley, Mayor Tom Pyne, CEO Bill Mills; (standing from left) deputy mayor Jeff Pezzutti, Graham Brasch, Angle Mustafa, Jan McLucas, Darren Cleland, Fran Lindsay, Annette Sheppard, Brian Down, Deirdre Ford, Sno Bonneau and Alan McPherson.

Chapter eight - 1990s

The major event of the 1990s was the amalgamation of Mulgrave Shire and the Cairns City into a single council with the election in March 1995 voting in former long-serving Mulgrave mayor Tom Pyne as the greater city's first mayor. Pyne served the introductory five-year term then moved on, leaving the way for Kevin Byrne to be elected in 2000 to the position he successfully recontested in 2004.

The first local authority in this area was the Cairns Road Board which functioned from the year of settlement in 1876 to 1879 when the Cairns Divisional Board was constituted. The Cairns Municipal Council was declared in 1885. It became the Cairns Town Council in 1903, then the Cairns City Council in 1923 when the population reached 8000 and so qualified to be known as a city.

The town (city) council boundary steadily moved outwards. Originally, it was a line through Fearnley St, a few metres west of the Cairns Showground, then to Chinaman Creek and later still out to Clarke Creek. The Cairns Divisional Board continued to operate from 1885, controlling the area outside the city boundary. It became the Cairns Shire Council in 1902, then the Mulgrave Shire Council from 1940. A Barron Divisional Board operated from 1890-1902 and then became the Barron Shire Council from 1902-19. Its area of control was brought back into the Cairns (later Mulgrave) Shire Council from 1919.

The mayor of Cairns during my early life was William Aloysius (Billy) Collins who still holds the record for the longest service in that position (1927-49). The Labor Party controlled the council during my early adult years. I did not know their first mayor, Bill Murchison, a railway porter who in 1949 unseated Billy Collins after his record run. But I did know Bill Fulton who took over as mayor in 1952 when Murchison died and served in the position until 1960. Fulton had a bicycle and sports shop in Shields St and was a fine rugby league player before World War II, during which he

John Cleland took over as mayor of Cairns when Keith Goodwin and deputy mayor Rose Blank were killed in an aircraft crash at Mt Emerald, near Tolga, on May 11, 1990. Ald Cleland, who owned a pharmacy in Mulgrave Rd and was chairman of the Cairns Cricket Association, died in office at Christmas 1991.

MAYORS OF CAIRNS

Louis Severin

1885-86: Richard Kingsford

1886-88: Louis Severin

1889: Richard Kingsford

1890: Callaghan Walsh

1891: Louis Severin

1891-93: A.J. Draper

1893-94: Daniel Patience

1895-96: James Lyons

1897: A.J. Draper

1898: Karl Aumuller

1899: Lyne Brown

1900-91: Richard Tills	1919: Richard Gelling
1902: A.J. Draper	1920: John Hoare
1903: Louis Severin	1921-24: John Hoare
1904: Donald McLachlan	1924-27: A.J. Draper
1905: Donald McKenzie	1927-49: William Collins
1906: Edward Earl	1949-52: William Murchison
1907: Richard Tills	1952-60: William Fulton
1908: Sinclair Miller	1960-67: Darcy Chataway
1909: John Coxall	*1967-69: Colin Penridge
1910: Andrew Hartill-Law	1969-73: Dave De Jarlais
1911: John Hoare	1973-76: Kevin Crathern
1912-13: Charles McKenzie	*1977-78: Dave de Jarlais
1914: Thomas Dillon	1978-88: Ron Davis
1915: John Griffiths	*1988-90: Keith Goodwin
1915-16: Thomas Dillon	*1990-91: John Cleland
1917: Thomas Donaldson	1992-95: Kevin Byrne
1918: A.J. Draper	1995-2000: Tom Pyne
	2000-: Kevin Byrne

One-year terms until 1921, then three-year terms until 1995 when Cairns City and Mulgrave Shire amalgamated for an initial five-year term. Four-year terms began in 2004.

* Died in office.

became one of the Rats of Tobruk. Fulton held the unusual distinction of being mayor and Labor's federal member for Leichhardt at the same time for some months in 1960 before Seymour Darcy Eagle Chataway, another railway worker, became the Labor mayor until he retired in 1967. It was then that Labor's long reign in Cairns City Council ended.

In the 1967 election for mayor, an independent, Colin Penridge, won a three-cornered contest against Basil Creedy (Labor) and Dave de Jarlais (Civic). Penridge led an eight-member council of four Civic aldermen, three Labor and one independent. I covered some council meetings in those times and Penridge tried to impose his influence on the divided council by starting meetings with the "mayor's minutes". A former railway stationmaster at Gordonvale, then Edge Hill shopkeeper and real estate agent, Penridge's supporters regarded him as a visionary. One of his ideas, which gained national publicity, was a proposal to import monkeys to be trained to pick coconuts from palms along the Esplanade and in parks so that locals and visitors would not be injured by falling nuts. But his council colleagues were unimpressed. Penridge died suddenly in office in August 1969.

Dave de Jarlais was elected mayor and won the next election in 1970, but suffered a shock loss in 1973 when Labor's Kev Crathern, one of the founders of Australian football in Cairns, won the mayoralty with a majority Labor council. But de Jarlais won office again in 1976 for the Civic team. A tireless worker for the community in many areas and long-time president of the Cairns Show Association, de Jarlais died suddenly in office on April 9, 1978. His deputy Ron Davis assumed the mayoralty and started a reign of 10 years for his Civic-controlled council. Davis and his council bore the brunt of the first wave of heavy demand for development in Cairns as tourism began to take off in the region. Long-time local residents began to express their disquiet about high-rise buildings spoiling the city's laidback lifestyle. Davis and his team were swept from office by a new force in local politics, the Alliance team which was a mix of Laborites and independents. The team was led by Keith

Goodwin who died in a plane crash near Atherton on May 11, 1990. John Cleland, who owned a pharmacy in Mulgrave Rd and was chairman of the Cairns Cricket Association, took over as mayor but he died in office at Christmas 1991. Kevin Byrne became mayor in a by-election against Labor's Desley Boyle, and then Byrne headed a new Unity team to win the election in 1994. I have never seen such a dramatic swing in voter support in such a short time in Cairns local government elections as in those held between 1988 and 1994. Goodwin led the new Alliance team to win the mayoralty and seven of the other eight seats in 1988, John Cleland won the mayoralty for Alliance and all other eight seats in 1991, but Alliance's appeal disintegrated so much over in-fighting and self-serving grandstanding by some of its members that it was wiped out when it lost the mayoralty to Kevin Byrne and all the other eight seats to Byrne's Unity team in 1994.

I am not sure what started the push for amalgamation of Mulgrave and Cairns, but I recall that a majority of North Queensland mayors supported some kind of rationalisation of boundaries at a local government conference in the early 1990s. It created some protest and expressions of concern about boundaries and possible job losses, but nothing like the widespread hysteria in August 2007 when the Beattie Labor Government accepted an independent commission's recommendation to reduce Queensland's local authorities from 156 to 72.

At the time of a review in 1994 by local government commissioner Greg Hoffman, Cairns city had a population of about 40,000 and Mulgrave shire 60,000. District residents were offered options such as Kuranda being included in either Mulgrave or Cairns, and Babinda going into the Johnstone Shire. However, residents of those towns voted overwhelmingly against change. Two Mulgrave councillors even suggested that the rapidly growing Marlin Coast area might become a separate local authority. Three in five of the 63 per cent of Cairns voters polled said they wanted some change. Eleven of 18 Cairns and Mulgrave councillors voted in favour of amalgamation in a public declaration of their

views. All eight Cairns councillors were in favour but only three of Mulgrave's 12 agreed.

Hoffman on September 27, 1994 recommended full amalgamation and on December 12, 1994, state cabinet approved the merger and set March 11, 1995 as the date for the election. In an 85 per cent turnout of voters, Tom Pyne won the mayoralty from Byrne 25,970 votes to 18,190 with four other candidates, and his Greater Cairns team took nine of the 12 seats contested by 36 candidates. Byrne's Unity team gained two places, and Sno Bonneau as an independent won the remaining seat. Cr Ross Parisi, the former Mulgrave councillor who had opposed the merger from the start, led a push in mid-1996 to try to have the amalgamation dismantled but a petition failed to gain the 10 per cent support of the 62,816 voters required to force a referendum.

The Cairns Post on March 25, 1995 published a feature article it had asked me to write on my observations of the two councils during my life. I nominated what I regarded as an ideal council from the former Cairns and Mulgrave councils, dubbed "The Dream Team" by the paper. It was Ron Davis (mayor), Keith Goodwin (deputy mayor), Jim Barlow, Rose Blank, John Cleland, Margaret Cossins, Dave de Jarlais, Henry Friend, Margaret Gill, Stan Marsh, Ross Parisi, Tom Pyne and Joan Wright.

Construction on the Reef Casino which opened on January 31, 1996 changed forever the precinct near the waterfront where the city's first buildings were erected soon after settlement in 1876. Most Cairns old-timers remember this part of the CBD for the Commonwealth Bank on the Spence-Abbott corner, the Koch memorial fountain in the centre of the intersection, Anzac Park and its band rotunda, a kiosk, the maternal welfare centre, and the Customs and other government buildings that occupied the site for much of the 20th century.

Another reason Anzac Park and the general precinct were so familiar to locals was that the buses which served Cairns in my childhood used the Abbott St frontage as their city

A big crowd of workers around the Anzac Park rotunda attend a meeting organised by the Trades & Labour Council during a strike in September 1961. Cairns bus services used the Abbott St frontage of Anzac Park as their city terminal, circa 1930s. The city site now is occupied by the Reef Casino with the Commonwealth Bank building in the foreground, circa 1940s.

terminal. They parked on an angle rear end into the kerb, between the Commonwealth Bank and the Customs building. I had a few trips in the late 1930s on the old Parramatta-West End bus (when we could afford it) for we lived for a while in Buchan St near today's Scott St roundabout. I remember that old bus, with its mainly wooden chassis, chugging along over the dusty (and at other times waterlogged), potholed gravel surfaces, in the days before the city's streets were paved with bitumen. Jack and Melva Walsh took over the Parramatta fleet around the mid-1950s.

Some of the other services in early days included George Metcalfe's red bus which ran along Martyn St to the Enmore area, Bill Watkins's Wattle bus which ran to Edge Hill along McLeod St, and Bill Simpson's Black & White buses which had the Abbott St to Edge Hill route. Edgar Williams, who lived in Cairns St, bought the service from Bill Watkins around 1950, and Alf White also operated the Phoenix bus service along McLeod St in earlier years.

When we went to town, we used to wait for the bus for the return home in Anzac Park, mothers resting with their bags of shopping on the benches under the huge mango trees while we took a turn on the swings and seesaws, or played on the band rotunda. Apart from being a popular play area for children, the rotunda, erected in the 1930s, was well used for brass band recitals in my younger days. I recall many a balmy Sunday evening in the 1950s sitting on a blanket in company with dozens of other families enjoying their music. Parts of the city's Anzac Day services were once held there, too. After the main service in the morning at the cenotaph at the intersection of Abbott and Shields streets, speakers and performers assembled on the Anzac Park band rotunda in the afternoon, usually with the three local bands, the Railway, Citizens and Salvation Army, playing in turn.

It is fitting that the facade of the old Customs building has been retained at the Abbott St entrance of the Reef Casino. The first Customs House, built there soon after settlement, became the focus of much of the township's early activity as it represented virtually all of the government services under the one roof. It served as the courthouse, marriages took place there, the first church services were held there,

and the divisional board (our first form of local government) held its first meeting in the courthouse on the reserve on July 20, 1880. In the early 1900s, the state government made better use of the site and in 1911 offices were located in a new building at the southern end of Abbott St for the harbourmaster and Department of Agriculture.

The Labour Department office, Commonwealth Employment Service and Department of Social Services all occupied space in this building in later years. The Customs residence gardens were often used for fetes, concerts and public events, and in the early 1900s the local council frequently asked the state government to convert the area for use as a public park. The request was repeatedly refused until after World War I when the suggestion that it be declared as Anzac Memorial Park was accepted.

The Commonwealth Bank took over the Queensland Government Savings Bank site in 1921. It erected a new building on the corner site and added extensions in the 1930s and 1950s. It remained there until after the bank moved to Lake St in 1973. There were few more recognisable buildings

Work in 1995 is well under way on construction of the Reef Casino which opened on January 31, 1996. The development changed forever the precinct near the waterfront where the city's first buildings were erected soon after settlement in 1876. This part of the CBD bounded by Spence, Abbott and Wharf streets was where most government buildings, including the Customs building retained in the middle of the picture, occupied the site for much of the 20th century. Another reason Anzac Park and the general precinct was so familiar to locals was that the buses which once serviced Cairns used the Abbott St frontage as their city terminal. They parked on an angle rear end into the kerb.

in Cairns in my youth than the Commonwealth Bank, and it attracted a stream of customers throughout the day when banking hours were 10am to 3pm. Most families had a savings account there and kids of my generation had a bank savings book. When we had any money to spare, our teacher took our deposits and entered them in our books at school on Monday morning every week. White was the fashionable dress option for bank employees and other professionals in those days. The bank's manager and his assistants were usually decked out in white suits, the other male employees wore white slacks and shirt with a dark tie, and women wore white frocks. The two-storey Maternal and Child Welfare building that was erected in the 1950s next to the bank in Abbott St was one of the last buildings to remain on the site before demolition and site works of the Reef Casino began in 1993, with completion in February 1996.

Skyrail, which has proved to be a world leader in its field, opened in Cairns on August 31, 1995. The original concept was conceived in 1987 and was followed by seven years of pre-construction feasibility studies, and consultation and approval processes with local, state and federal governments and local communities. Work began in June 1994. Despite protests by environmental groups and concerned citizens about possible damage to the rainforest, Skyrail's operation has proved their fears were unfounded. Tower sites were selected to coincide with existing canopy gaps, and were surveyed to ensure no rare, threatened or endangered species would be affected by construction. Leaf litter and topsoil was collected and stockpiled for reintroduction when construction was complete. Plant seedlings were catalogued at each site, then removed and propagated during construction, and re-planted in their original locations, with the saved topsoil and leaf litter, when construction was complete. Helicopters were used extensively to assist construction, carrying equipment, materials and cement to tower sites and rainforest stations.

At a cost of $35 million, Skyrail opened to the public with 47 gondolas, giving it a carrying capacity of 300 people per hour. A $2.5 million upgrade completed in May 1997

Ken Chapman (left) with National Trust chairperson Petrina Ferrari and architect Roger Mainwood at the opening of the $33 million Skyrail project on August 31, 1995.

increased the gondolas to 114 and carrying capacity to 700 people an hour. Stretching 7.5km, Skyrail was the world's longest gondola cableway at the time of completion. It provided people with a unique opportunity – and a world first – to see and experience the rainforest in a safe and environmentally friendly way. In 2007, it remained the most environmentally sensitive cableway project in the world.

In May 1996, Skyrail won the Greening of Business Tourism Award for "most environmentally conscious visitor attraction" presented at the European Business Travel and Meetings Exhibition in Geneva. It has won several Queensland and Australian tourism and environmental awards since. Skyrail chairman and owner George Chapman received an award in recognition of his efforts and achievements to Australian tourism.

Skyrail's operation complements the popular Kuranda Scenic Rail trip, which was constructed more than a century before during five years of incredible physical effort and human sacrifice from 1887 to 1891. It was officially recognised by Engineers Australia at a ceremony at Kuranda on September 3, 2005 as one of the greatest engineering feats in this nation's history. That 24.5km section of rail line up the range was built at a cost of about $110 million in today's values and at least 26 men who were known to have lost their lives during construction. The contract required construction of 15 tunnels (19 were originally planned) totalling 2138m in length; 55 bridges, some made of wood and others of steel; and more than 1250 cuttings. Some had to be built so that they perched precariously over deep ravines and waterfalls. Extensive excavations were necessary for many tunnels and cuttings on dangerous bends as the route snaked around 98 curves in the 24.5km section. The Kuranda Scenic Rail has proved to be one of the great train rides of the world. Construction of the line, 40 years before the coastal railway from Brisbane to Cairns was completed in 1926, came about by a state government keen to consolidate a shaky hold on northern electorates after agitation by the rich mining region centred on Herberton, in the upper Atherton Tablelands,

Opening of the Tjapukai cultural park at Smithfield in July 1996 provided one of the most popular tourist attractions that Cairns has introduced in Alan Hudson's lifetime. It was an extension of the Tjapukai dance theatre founded in Kuranda in 1987.

Bob Norman, founder of Bush Pilots Airways in the early 1950s, whose generous financial support led to the opening of James Cook University's campus at Smithfield in 1986.

for a reliable means of transport to connect it to the coast. With construction from Cairns starting in May 1886, it was eventually completed to Herberton in October 1910. The story of this fascinating project is told in *Tracks of Triumph*, a book that I researched and wrote, which was published by The Cairns Post Pty Ltd in November 2003.

The Cairns Campus of James Cook University will remain a Cairns landmark as a reminder of the contribution to this community by Sir Bob Norman, who died in Cairns on April 3, 2007, aged 93. JCU has named its new Australian Tropical Forest Institute Building completed in 2007 the Sir Robert Norman Building in recognition of his significant role in the development of the campus. In his pragmatic way of dealing with what he saw as important issues for the betterment of the Cairns community, Sir Robert said in 2003 about his involvement with JCU: "Our own daughters had to go away to Brisbane to study, and

we wanted to give students those opportunities locally: we wanted to keep our talented young people in the Far North."

When it was announced in 1986 that JCU was to establish a campus at the Cairns College of Technical and Further Education, the Norman family and other local campaigners remained convinced that Cairns needed its own university, able to offer a wide range of courses. At the formal announcement of the opening of the Cairns campus of JCU at TAFE, Sir Robert and Lady Norman presented a $100,000 donation towards the establishment of a university campus in Cairns. The family later increased their commitment to $250,000 and Sir Robert became the chair of the Cairns Campus Co-ordinating Committee which raised almost $1 million to purchase the land on which JCU Cairns now stands. In July 1995, JCU Cairns officially opened its own campus at Smithfield, with 900 students and 50 staff.

There has been continuing expansion of existing activities as well as initiation of new projects. In 2003, a new Health

Sciences precinct at JCU Cairns was officially opened, enabling JCU Cairns to play an increasing role in activities associated with the development of JCU's medical school, as well as expand its science offerings. Sir Robert Norman's aim to keep our young people in the Far North has been realised as about 80 per cent of JCU's students come from North Queensland, studying in its main campuses at Townsville and Cairns. JCU Cairns enrolments in 2007 exceeded 3300.

Sir Robert was a World War II bomber pilot and founder of Bush Pilots Airways in Cairns in 1951. The airline grew out of a mercy flight on January 22 that year by the young Bob Norman to Cargoon, a Hughenden cattle station owned by Bev Anning, one of North Queensland's best-known graziers. Anning's wife was seriously ill and needed to be airlifted to hospital from their flooded property. Norman landed his Tiger Moth on a makeshift landing strip nearby. Norman was convinced by that single incident that formation of a regular aerial service to the outback was essential.

With the support of Anning and other graziers, Bush

Pilots Airways was born. By the 1970s, it had become Australia's biggest country airline.

The need for more bike lanes in Cairns during the 1990s to meet a resurgence of interest in cycling provoked memories of my more youthful years when bicycles were the main means of transport for locals. Bicycles now are used mainly for leisure, or for the more vigorous disciplines of BMX, mountain biking and triathlons, whereas in my younger days, when two-car families would have been laughed at as an impossible dream, bicycles were an essential means of transport and outnumbered the four-wheelers on Cairns streets. The biggest employers in Cairns had extensive bike racks on their premises so workers could park their wheels for the day. But they were a luxury for some families. I, and most of my mates, did not have a bike through all of our schooldays. We walked everywhere. I bought my first bicycle about a year after I started work in January 1947 from Wally Foulger, who set up Trinity Cycle Works in 1938,

Bosanko's in Aplin St was one of several bike shops in the city in the 1930s-50s when most Cairns people used bicycles as their principal means of transport.

a business still trading in 2007 under that name at 40 Aplin St. Wally had several shops over the years in that area and he was operating from 25 Aplin St when I bought my bike from him. With a population of under 15,000 in the 1940s, Cairns had at least six other shops that I recall: Fulton's at 62c Shields St, Malvern Star (20 Shields), Eddlestons (111 Lake), Noxall Motors (103 Lake), Harris Cycle Works (94 Lake), and Bosankos (34 Aplin).

One of the earliest bicycle retailers in Cairns was probably Massey Harris Cycle Depot owned by Frederick George Locke in Lake St. It was founded before World War I and was still trading in the 1920s. Francis Ireland, founder of the Cairns motor dealer that still bears his name, started his working life as a bicycle repairer and later opened his first business, Ireland and Daniel, in the 1920s selling and repairing bicycles and motorcycles. He graduated to motor vehicles when he secured the Chrysler franchise.

George Harris was one of Francis Ireland's mechanic workmates in those early years, and Harris later set up what was to become one of the best-known bicycle sales and repair shops in Cairns. Harris started his business beneath the family home at 345 Sheridan St, and opened his first shop at the western end of Shields St before moving to Lake St, opposite today's Commonwealth Bank, with his younger brother Les working for him. After World War II, George Harris bought the premises at 94 Lake St, known then as Page's building, and eventually sold the business to Les. Many Cairns people of my generation remember Harris Cycle Works where they parked their bikes at night while they went to the Tropical and Palace pictures, or dances at the Aquatic and Trocadero. In the 1940s, it cost sixpence to leave a bike at Harris's for safe-keeping. The busiest night was Saturday when up to 100 machines would be left there, with Tuesday the slowest night when 40 customers were the average.

Bosanko's Cycle Works, at 34 Aplin St, had the agency for Brittania bicycles and were also gunsmiths. Harry Bosanko, or Bowey as everyone knew him, was a stalwart of the brass band movement in Cairns and was a great mate of Bert Butler, one of the city's long-standing hairdressers. Malvern Star, the company formed in Melbourne by Bruce Small, later to become the driving force in the development of the Gold Coast, had a shop at 20 Shields St. In 1947, Malvern Star in Cairns advertised ladies and gents bicycles from £12 (about $650 today), payable at four shillings and sixpence a week.

Bill Fulton, a representative rugby league player in the 1930s and one of the Rats of Tobruk during World War II, had his cycle works and sports shop at 62c Shields St, opposite the Crown Hotel. Fulton, who became mayor of Cairns from 1952-60, then the Labor member for Leichhardt, regularly advertised in *The Cairns Post* a service for replacing tyres on prams, trikes and scooters.

Eddlestons was founded in the 1920s by William R. Eddleston at 111 Lake St. I remember going there often in the early 1950s to inflate my tyres from the free air pump down the lane at the side of the premises. Eddleston's sons, Ralph and Albert, were partners in the business and later Gordon Holden, the firm's bookkeeper, was taken in as a partner. Holden took over the business in the 1950s and transferred the operations to 47 Lake St where it continued until it closed in 1979. Eddlestons had the agency for Excelsior bicycles, and Harley Davidson, BSA, Norton and Acme motorcycles, and Bill McGregor, who later had his own business in McLeod St for many years, was one of the motorcycle mechanics. Ron Mercer, who later opened his own cycle business in Sheridan St near the Cairns High School, worked there as the bicycle repairer.

Cairns in the early 1990s had continued to enjoy buoyant times on the back of the surge in tourist numbers since the mid-1980s when Cairns International Airport opened. But then from the mid-1990s the city began one of the biggest financial downturns I have known in my adult life. It was a time that an old friend and local economist Bill Cummings described to me as Cairns's worst economic slump since the late 1960s. Annual growth during this time dropped to a low of 0.5 per cent when peaks

A huge crowd on the Esplanade in the 1990s for the Fun in the Sun Festival which had its origins at the opening of a new Green Island jetty on May 28, 1962. About 10,000 people watched a procession more than 3km long. Festivities included 111 floats and 1700 participants in various roles including clowns, horseback riders, decorated bikes, bands, marching girls and brass bands. Mayor Darcy Chataway said at the time: "I trust that every year from now on Cairns will have a procession and festival: our own week."

in the good times had achieved highs of 5 per cent. Recovery did not begin until 2002.

Cummings said a building boom had reached saturation point around 1996 after high dwelling construction in 1994-95. By the next year, it had overshot demand. Property prices peaked in 1994 and then began to fall away in a sluggish property market of which I had first-hand experience. My wife Hilary and I were thinking at this time of moving to an Esplanade unit, but it was conditional on being able to sell our home. It was a neat three-bedroom home on a large corner block in Edge Hill. Our agent held an open house one weekend and we advertised it in *The Cairns Post* several times. But we did not have a single inquiry or an inspection over a period of some weeks and we eventually withdrew it from sale. I am sure we would have had no trouble selling it a decade later at twice the price we had it offered.

Cairns hotels experienced a drop in room occupancy rates around this time among complaints about costs of airfares and accommodation. Japanese visitor numbers stopped growing and soon started to fall off. A slide in the value of the region's mining production which would last for four years contributed to the gloomy economic situation.

The slump reached its low in 2000-01 when construction activity was valued at only $250 million, down 60 per cent on its 1994-95 peaks. It was then that the situation began to turn around as agricultural production continued to grow, mining production rallied, and the Japanese tourist market revived after the Asian investment crisis and started to move strongly upwards. Airport passenger numbers moved up in 2001-02 and construction and population growth started to increase again. Other major events that cast a gloom over the world and had an impact on slowing the economic recovery

The Cairns Convention Centre opened on July 20, 1996. The centre was voted in 2004 by convention planners as the world's best venue and again in 2005 as one of the world's top three venues. In June 2007, it brought $16.5 million into the local economy when 3500 delegates attended functions there.

in the Cairns region included the 9/11 (September 11, 2001) terrorist attack on New York's World Trade Centre. Who will ever forget watching those images on television of the planes crashing into the twin towers? I recall sitting in my lounge room at home around 6.30am, my mouth agape thinking for a while that I surely must be watching some fanciful Hollywood movie instead of real life in all of its horror.

The collapse of Ansett's airline in March 2002, the Bali bombing of October 2, 2002, the SARS (severe acute respiratory syndrome) pandemic from November 2002, which caused more than 760 deaths in China and other East Asian countries, and the start of the Iraq war in March 2003 were other factors which contributed to the economic woes.

But Cairns began its economic fight back in the early 2000s. The Chamber of Commerce produced in January 2003 a report to be used as a marketing tool that tagged it the "City of Opportunity". Chamber executive officer Sandy Whyte announced, "We've weathered the storm. We are now gearing back up to where we were a few years ago." He said much of the potential for business growth was related to Cairns's increasing role as an aviation hub for international and domestic travel. Cairns was seen as a safe destination by

overseas travellers wary of terrorism since 9/11 and the 2002 Bali bombing. Domestic tourists looked to Cairns as a cheap destination after being scared off by high currency exchange rates in Europe. One advantage of the economic downturn was seen as a culling-out of the weaker businesses in the Cairns region. Those left were "lean and mean" and well-placed to take advantage of future growth.

The Cairns Post reported in August 2003 that the Far North's economy was in good shape again with tourism recovering from SARS and the building sector at full capacity. The paper cited a Herron Todd White monthly CairnsWatch report which said local employment levels had slowed down in June, attributed to a delayed reaction to SARS and the invasion of Iraq. But it said the tourism downturn was on the mend. International arrivals were expected to reach normal by September of that year. Supply of new housing was being hampered by a building industry already working to full capacity as approvals reached 125 dwellings in May and flattened out to 95. Overall, business confidence was optimistic but cautious, the newspaper report said, with the seventh consecutive positive confidence index since the Ansett collapse.

MOMENTS IN TIME

1990 – March
End of pilots' strike (started August 24, 1989), costing estimated $60 million to local economy.

1990 – March 10
New Cairns post office and mail sorting complex opens in Grafton St.

1991 – May 11
Hambledon sugar mill at Edmonton crushes its last cane after 109 years.

1991 – September 14
Esplanade night markets and food court open.

1991 – December 25
Cairns mayor John Cleland dies in office.

1992 – November 20
Police station and courthouse complex opens in Grafton St.

1993 – February
Kamerunga Research Station closes after 104 years.

1993 – August 29
Historic House on the Hill destroyed by fire.

1993 – October 15-24
Operation Trek Back, 50th reunion of World War II service personnel who served in district.

1995 – March 11
First election for merged Cairns and Mulgrave councils with former Mulgrave mayor Tom Pyne as first mayor.

1995 – July 15
Cairns Regional Gallery opens in Abbott St in former Public Curator building.

1995 – August 31
$33 million Skyrail trip over rainforest from Smithfield to Kuranda, opens.

1995 – September 18
City's first internet cafe opens in Sheridan St at Rick's Place, opposite Cairns State High School.

1995 – December 6
Cairns campus of James Cook University opens at Smithfield with 900 enrolments.

1996 – January 31
Cairns Reef Casino opens on site of former Anzac Park.

1996 – May 7
McLeod St railway station relocates to Bunda St.

1996 – July 8
Tjapukai Cultural Park opens at Smithfield.

1996 – July 20
New Cairns Convention Centre opens in Wharf St.

1996 – October 6-20
Fun in the Sun and Dive festivals combine to form Reef festival.

1997 – August
Cairns Central opens on site of former Cairns railway station in McLeod St.

1998 – October 2
New council chambers occupied in Spence St.

The former Public Curator building, which opened as the Cairns Regional Gallery on July 15, 1995.

Opening of the Esplanade Lagoon in March 2003 has provided Cairns with the city's most popular public amenities.

Chapter nine - 2000s

The Esplanade has been the city's most popular promenade and leisure spot for more than a century. Families relaxed there as early as the 1880s and ladies paraded wearing their ankle length gowns, lace-up boots and bonnets. It had been surveyed by John Sharkey soon after settlement in 1876 to about 40m from high water mark. Its concrete retaining wall was thought to have been constructed in the 1890s. The Esplanade Lagoon, officially opened on the weekend of March 29-20, 2003, has been one of the most successful public amenities I have seen in this city in my lifetime, supported so well with that wonderful boardwalk the length of the seafront, the barbecues and other public facilities and playground equipment. This work has complemented the extensive landscaping and beautification of the Esplanade that were undertaken by Mayor Ron Davis's council back in the late 1970s and early 1980s.

The Esplanade Lagoon has taken its place in our community more than a century after safe swimming enclosures were exercising the minds of our civic leaders. Bathing in unauthorised public places was frowned upon at this time. In February 1904, three men were charged with bathing in a public place, in the long-since reclaimed Alligator Creek off Bunda St. However, police were unsure if the local council had an appropriate bylaw in place prohibiting public bathing and the case was dismissed.

The first public swimming pool in Cairns was officially opened by mayor Louis Severin on February 25, 1888. Built in 1888 by the Cairns Floating Baths Co. Limited, they were at the southern end of Lake St long before the present concrete wharves were built. The baths were about 22m by 8m and varied in depth from 1m to a little over 2m. Pontoons supported them so that they could float up and down with

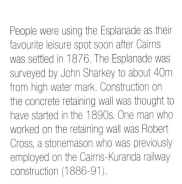

People were using the Esplanade as their favourite leisure spot soon after Cairns was settled in 1876. The Esplanade was surveyed by John Sharkey to about 40m from high water mark. Construction on the concrete retaining wall was thought to have started in the 1890s. One man who worked on the retaining wall was Robert Cross, a stonemason who was previously employed on the Cairns-Kuranda railway construction (1886-91).

the tides. Although popular enough with locals, the wooden structure was always in need of repair and partly sank in February 1890 when the company proposed putting them up for auction. The next public baths were located at the end of a jetty off the Esplanade where the Hilton Hotel is now. They were opened in 1903 and the first swimming carnival was held in April 1904. The floating baths operated from this location for many years until they were demolished during the 1920 cyclone. The wooden structure was swept out to sea. They were eventually rebuilt and reopened on November 15, 1921. Several other makeshift private swimming enclosures off the Esplanade, constructed mainly of wire-netting, were used by Cairns people in the 1920s.

Three pools operated at one time, one in front of the hospital, another outside the RSL, and the third was attached to a pontoon in front of the former Pacific Hotel. These various enclosures off the Esplanade were known by the locals as "mud pools". The Cairns Amateur Swimming and Rowing Club was formed in March 1919.

The first concrete baths in Cairns were opened on May 9, 1931 with their entrance in Wharf St about where today's Hilton Hotel is. I learned to swim there in the 1930s. The pool was filled with seawater. It was flushed every day, and emptied and refilled every 48 hours. Fred Robinson was well known as the baths manager. He served in the position from 1938 until they closed in 1962. The first major swimming meet held there was the North Queensland titles in 1933. The old Esplanade pool, where hundreds of Cairns people spent many pleasant hours, closed during construction of the Tobruk Memorial Pool at North Cairns which opened on March 24, 1962. For a few years, the old site operated as an oceanarium.

When I was in scholarship class at Parramatta State School in 1944, my good mate Ron Beecheno one day told me we should start going to church every Sunday. At age 13, Ron solemnly announced from that day on we were turning over a new leaf, and there would be

The original Anglican Church was located in Abbott St, next to today's City Library. It was taken over by the Cairns and District Masonic Club in 1924 and they installed a lawn bowling green at the street frontage. The club upgraded its premises on the site in the 1960s and it later became the Cairns City Club which closed early in 2006. The Hedley Group's Centrepoint Apartments building was being constructed there in the second half of 2007.

no more swearing or salacious thoughts. So it was off to St Johns Anglican Church in Lake St every Sunday for Ron and me. It was one of the rare occasions in my childhood when I wore shoes and socks.

It was not long before we were enrolled in the confirmation class for that year with a view to taking our first communion a few months later. My bachelor uncle, John Kelly, a wharf labourer who lived only a block away from us in Hartley St, took me in hand one afternoon after school and we went to Eddie Deeb's store at 31a Shields St where John bought me a new navy serge suit (with short trousers), a gleaming white shirt and a patterned red and blue tie to wear for the occasion. And so I took my first communion one evening with 58 other pious young Cairns adolescents. One of that communion class was George Tung Yep.

It would have been absurd to have suggested then that 60 or so years forward I would be sitting with my wife Hilary at St Johns sharing with a happy congregation a celebration of 50 years of wonderful service to the priesthood by George who some years earlier had been installed Bishop of Cairns. That joyous occasion was in February 2005. George shares with St Johns the same birth year of 1927.

The Anglican Church in Cairns traces its beginnings to 1877 when services were first held in the Customs bond store at the southern end of Abbott St. The first St Johns was built on a block of land in Abbott St on a site just a few doors south of today's City Library. Rev. J. Webber held the Palm Sunday services in the new church for the first time in April 1984. That building was demolished in the cyclone of February 2, 1920, and a fundraising drive was held to rebuild St Johns on a new site at its present location on the corner of Lake and Minnie streets. The foundation stone of the second St Johns was laid on June 27, 1926. The new St Johns church was dedicated on January 23, 1927. St Johns has not only been the place of worship for many Cairns citizens, but a centre of social, community and sporting activity.

The Cairns and District Masonic Club soon after took over the old 137 Abbott St site and on July 26, 1924 it opened

Bishop George Tung Yep, who celebrated 50 years of priesting in 2003, was a member of St Johns Anglican Church's 1944 communion class with Alan Hudson and 58 others.

its clubhouse in a building that was previously the Anglican rectory and later set down a lawn bowling green fronting the street. The bowls club moved to a new location in Grove St in 1962. The club upgraded the site as its licensed premises. It later became the Cairns City Club which closed early in 2006. The Hedley Group's multi-storey Centrepoint apartments building was being completed on this site in the second half of 2007.

Cyclones are the nightmare that every Far North Queenslander lives with during summer months. I unashamedly confess to being terrified by their mere presence off the coast, after having lived through three major cyclones that have hit this region and several more that have threatened the stretch of coastline where we live.

I experienced my first devastating cyclone when Agnes came to town on March 6, 1956. Agnes, a Category 3 cyclone (170-224km/h), was unusual, and probably unique, for a couple of reasons: its wide scope of influence from well south of Townsville area north to Cairns, and that it was "dry" with its winds of up to 150 km/h whipping up clouds of sand and dust. Agnes crossed the coast in the Burdekin area at 3pm on a Tuesday. It damaged almost every building in the township of Ayr. It proceeded north to Ingham where it turned inland and then made its way south until it became a rain depression.

Jeff Callaghan, an authority on tropical cyclones at the Bureau of Meteorology in Brisbane, explained why Cairns suffered so much damage when the cyclone centre was over Townsville: "Agnes was unusual. It had a big open centre and its circulation was very large. As it straddled the coast the winds spread, and Cairns suffered more damage than Townsville. Westerly winds coming from the downslope of the hills behind Cairns gusted from zero to more than 80 knots and this (gusting) factor put terrible stress on structures". Cyclone warnings then were not as sophisticated as today. City workers heard Agnes was threatening the central Queensland coast as we went off to work on that Tuesday morning. When winds started to build up, workers

headed for home around mid-morning to try to secure their properties. Shops and other businesses closed. By noon, the city was almost deserted, except for essential services such as police, fire brigade and ambulance, some staff at *The Cairns Post* and the telegraph office in Spence St now occupied by Ken Done. Remarkably, the Tropical Theatre in Abbott St went ahead with its afternoon matinee. Even more remarkably, 12 patrons sat through the two movies, *Bedevilled* starring Anne Baxter and *Down to the Sea in Ships* with Richard Widmark.

We felt our relatively new home in Jones St, off Mulgrave Rd, was vulnerable as the front porch area had not been enclosed. The cyclone's full force struck around midnight. My wife and I, with two pre-school children, had an anxious night, expecting at any time to lose a sheet or two of roofing iron or have windows blasted in. But we were lucky. The house escaped structural damage. Our main problem the next day was sweeping out the piles of sand that had worked its way under the doors.

Not so lucky were my good friends Linde and Shirley Allendorf, who have lived at Woree for many years. The Allendorfs lost a new home they would have moved to a few days later in Ward St, near Balaclava State School. A positive outcome for the Allendorfs was that they had insured the home for £2800 (about $90,000 today) only two weeks before. "That's the best wager I've ever had," said Linde Allendorf, a noted racing man as a former local jockey and trainer. Dozens of other Cairns people had their homes destroyed or severely damaged. Scarcely a building along Mulgrave Rd was spared some damage and many were levelled. Four wartime igloos in Aumuller St and another along Mulgrave Rd were among the buildings that had collapsed. Many Cairns people were left homeless. Temporary accommodation for 700 was provided in the Migrant Centre in Hartley St and the YAL in Martyn St.

I have often said that no one deserves to experience more than one damaging cyclone in their lifetime. But Innisfail district people, within two decades, took the brunt of two of the most devastating cyclones ever to have hit the Far North.

Cairns was on the fringe of Cyclone Winifred but it was enough for locals to appreciate its devastating force. It struck the Innisfail district around 7pm on Saturday, February 1, 1986. While Cairns and other regional centres felt its effects, its main area of impact was from Babinda to Mission Beach. Winds gusted to 240km/h and dumped some 380mm of rain in 24 hours. The cyclone caused three deaths: a man died at Malanda when he was blown off the roof of his house while undertaking repairs, a young girl in Innisfail died after being injured by roofing iron blown through the window of a house, and a man drowned in a flooded storm drain near Ingham. Damage to buildings and crops was estimated at $400 million (in 2007 values). Winifred left in its wake an eerie landscape with thousands of trees of all sizes denuded of their leaves, including most of the rainforest areas and pine plantations. Many trees were either uprooted or had their trunks and limbs snapped off by the huge winds.

Cyclone Larry, a few weeks more than 20 years later, hit the same area around daybreak on Monday, March 20, 2006 with the most destructive force ever experienced in the Far North in my lifetime. Winds were thought to have been up to 290km/h. However, it was later described as a "marginal" Category 5 (280km/h and over) and the wind gusts estimated as up to 240km/h (Category 4). Miraculously, there was no loss of life. My wife Hilary and I have a second home at Kurrimine Beach, about 30km south of Innisfail. We were there some 16 hours before the cyclone's landfall and it was inconceivable on one of the loveliest Sundays we had experienced all summer that such a force was on its way. Although our house escaped major structural damage, we saw how destructive that Larry was to people's lives, and the buildings, crops and the environment generally in its relatively short, sharp rush across the Tully to Babinda area and through to the southern Tablelands region. Hardly a building between Tully and Babinda escaped some structural and/or water damage and most of it was severe. On the coast, banana plantations were destroyed and cane crops flattened.

Cyclone Agnes (category 3) on March 6, 1956 caused widespread destruction in the Cairns district, including this wartime "igloo" warehouse in Mulgrave Rd that housed Pioneer tour buses, opposite today's Westcourt Plaza. Four other igloos built during World War II in Aumuller St were among the many buildings destroyed in Cairns.

One of the most heartwarming stories to come out of the disastrous aftermath of Cyclone Larry was the community support that led to the reopening of Fred and Carmel Lizzio's Munro Theatre at Babinda after it had been completely destroyed on March 20, 2006.

Tableland crops were extensively damaged. Stands of forest were laid bare with even the largest trees stripped of their leaves. Road and rail access to the region was disrupted for several days due to flooding. Townships were isolated. Food drops were required. Electricity transmission as far north as Cairns was severely disrupted. I will never forget the Ergon Energy workmen, toiling away for long hours in the oppressive humidity, patiently handling the countless requests from householders wondering when their supply would be restored, or the house-to-house drops of food and bottled water from volunteers.

It is impossible to put a definite value on the destruction caused by Larry although one report put the cost to the region as in the vicinity of $1.5 billion. I could not attempt to record here the damage in detail, or to adequately describe how the people pulled together during this terrible time, as well as the many acts of selfless behaviour by volunteer workers and others. It was an example of the wonderful reliance of Far Northerners and how they respond quite heroically when they are faced with adversity. I know it was of little comfort to people living in emergency shelters after their homes were destroyed, but I believe the ever-visible presence of community leaders like General Peter Cosgrove and Johnstone mayor Neil Clarke did much to lift the morale of Innisfail district people during Larry's long and distressing aftermath.

There were dozens of heartwarming stories from throughout the region in the wake of Larry, neighbour helping neighbour, complete strangers offering assistance, badly-hit shop-owners ignoring their own plight and giving away free food and other goods, and former residents coming back to the district after many years to contribute their special trade skills in the recovery process. One of my favourite stories was the restoration of the Munro Theatre in Babinda, owned by local pharmacist Fred Lizzio. Fred had operated the theatre three nights a week for the previous 25 years, not as a money-making venture but mainly as a community service.

He responded to pleas from local children to rebuild the theatre which had been completely destroyed. He was overcome by offers of help to clear the rubble and rebuild, and paid a special tribute to Cairns builder Brendan Canning who installed a new roof at a cost that made the whole rebuilding project viable. A $250,000 government grant and the community's fundraising efforts provided further help. The theatre's reopening on Saturday, June 2, 2007, was a grand day for Babinda and a shining example of how community spirit can overcame the ravages of disasters like Cyclone Larry.

The response and the exposure to the general public of these natural disasters so many years apart were varied. There was no State Emergency Service with Agnes in 1956. People were largely left to their own devices and the community generally relied upon the council and essential services like the police, fire brigade and ambulance. Of course, we had no television when Agnes hit Cairns and it was left to newspapers and radio to convey information to those who suffered damage and reports to the outside world. Winifred in February 1986 received wider coverage through the electronic media, and the events surrounding Larry in March 2006 were even more widely exposed with the situation appearing on television screens throughout Australia every day for many weeks afterwards.

The dominant theme during the last few years of the life of this book has been the phenomenal growth of Cairns. I have lost count of the number of people, including old-time locals, frequent visitors and former residents, who have told me they could not believe how much the city has changed. That is not surprising with the Cairns CBD these days catering mainly to the tourist trade with duty free shops, footpath eateries, internet cafes, jewellers, dive shops, reef and other tour operators and various tourist outlets where most of the city's business and commerce took place a generation or so ago.

The biggest change for me has been that transformation in the character of the CBD. Once, almost every service

This building on the corner of Aplin and Abbott streets, occupied by the National Motor Service in the 1920s, is almost as old as Cairns itself. It was gutted by fire three times but rebuilt each time as the same basic structure. It started life in the early 1890s as Alfred Taylor's plumbing works. Horrie Kennedy in 1929 bought the business that was trading as City Electric Light and remodelled it as his electrical showroom and workshop. It was gutted by fire in 1929, 1946 and 1984 and rebuilt every time. It was occupied by Kennedys until the firm transferred in September 1989 to McLeod St. Johnos Blues Bar was its occupant for many years until closing in May 2007.

that residents required was confined to the area bounded by McLeod, Spence, Abbott and Shields streets. All professional services, banks, motor dealers, wholesale merchants, some butchers, and the main grocery and clothing retailers were to be found in the CBD. It was also possible to visit the premises of a plumber or a bicycle repair shop in Lake St, a building contractor in Spence St, a foundry or an iceworks in Sheridan St, coach builder in McLeod St, cordial manufacturer on the Esplanade, and have a game of lawn bowls at 139 Abbott St. Cairns Fire Brigade was in Lake St where the public parking station is now, and Cairns ambulance was on the corner of Grafton and Aplin streets.

For years in the early part of my life, all our doctors, dentists, lawyers and accountants were in the main part of the CBD. Solicitors MacDonnell, Harris & Bell (still practising today as MacDonnells), Joe Bennett and O'Beirne & McNamee, had their offices alongside one another at 26-30 Abbott St. Murray Lyons were around the corner at 21

Spence St and Eric Dann, the doyen of the legal fraternity, had his offices upstairs at 22 Shields St. R.H. Crust, W. Smith & Co. and E.M. Boden, the city's main public accountants, were within arm's reach of one another in Abbott St, with Jim Tennant at 19 Spence St, Arthur Hooper at 79a Lake St and Kerr Tadman at 51 Lake St.

Our doctors, Tom Gregg, Bruce Clarke, D.C.C. Sword, Charles Mansfield, Bruce Clarke, Charles Knott and Les Westaway, all had their rooms in Abbott St, between Shields and Florence streets. Dentists George Brooks (75 Lake St), Jim Lander (21 Spence St), Les O'Brien (36 Abbott St) and Carl Knudson (121 Abbott St) were close by.

Many people lament the fact that development over the past two decades has destroyed much of our built history with multi-storey office and accommodation buildings popping up everywhere in the CBD. But I point out to them that much of our past has been retained, and for that I am thankful. The Cairns City Council has published a Heritage Walk brochure

which lists the following remaining sites of historical significance:
• School of Arts (now Cairns Museum in City Place, established in 1907);
• Hides Corner (est. 1885 and remodelled 1930);
• Lannoy House (Mazlin's Corner, 1927-28);
• Palace Theatre (Lake St, 1913);
• Clauson House (Shields St);
• Qantas building (Lake St, former W.A. Collins chemist, 1923);
• Central School (now Oasis Resort, 1884);
• City Council Chambers (now City Library, 1930);
• Alfred Taylor's (until May 2007 a nightclub, 1890);
• Cairns Regional Gallery (formerly Public Curator, 1934).
• Court House (Abbott St, 1919);
• The Cairns Post (Abbott St, 1908);
• Keeble's Building (Abbott St, 1926);
• Maritime House (or Howard Smith building in Abbott St, 1914);
• Post Office (corner Spence and Abbott streets, 1937);
• Telegraph Office (Spence St, 1928);
• Bolands original store (Spence St, 1902);
• Earl Court (formerly National Bank corner Lake and Spence streets, 1926);
• Boland Centre (1912);
• Central Hotel (corner Lake and Spence streets, 1909);
• Quaid Real Estate (formerly Adelaide Steamship Co., corner Lake and Spence streets, 1910).

I am surprised that 51 The Esplanade, the offices of Tourism Tropical North Queensland, is not included in the list. This was the original Cairns (later Mulgrave) Shire offices, built in 1912. Profit from the sale of the Cairns-Mulgrave Tramway (about $2.6 million in today's dollars) was used to build the shire offices. The tramway, which ran from Cairns to Babinda, was built and operated, profitably, by the Cairns Divisional Board, forerunner of the Cairns City Council, from 1897 until the Queensland Government took it over in 1912. The tramway's terminus was across the road

from today's Cape York Hotel on a site where GHD Pty Ltd's multi-storey office building was opened at 85 Spence St in 2006. The hotel was named the Tramway when it was built in 1898, became the National in 1926, and was renamed Cape York in 1987. The Cape York, as well as the Crown, Grand, Railway, Shenannigans (formerly Commercial) and Barrier Reef (formerly the Empire) hotels, are among other buildings that, although renovated at various times, still bear the same basic appearances as they were almost a century ago.

Most of present church buildings in the city also deserve to be recognised as part of the city's heritage. St John's Anglican Church in Lake St was occupied in the 1920s, St Andrews Presbyterian was built in Sheridan St in 1905 and replaced by a new building in 1953, and St Joseph's Catholic Church was established in 1928. St Monica's Catholic Church was established in Minnie St in 1886. The building was still being used in 2007 after the new cathedral in Abbott St was built in 1967-68. Bishop's House, on the corner of Minnie and Abbott streets, St Monica's Convent and the adjoining school were all established about a century ago and are important parts of our city's built history.

Cairns Base Hospital looks nothing like its original, established in 1884, but it still rates as a site of historical merit. More buildings were added in 1912. Cairns Private on the corner of Abbott and Upward streets, although it has been completely rebuilt, has an interesting history. Previously Calvary Hospital, it was originally built as the home of a prominent Cairns solicitor, Abijah Murray, in the early 1900s, and named Embo. The home is forever linked with one of Australia's great maritime tragedies when the steamer Yongala went missing off the coast near Townsville in March 1912. All 121 passengers and crew on board perished, and Murray lost all of his family: his wife and four children who had been holidaying in Sydney where Mrs Murray gave birth to the youngest, a girl. Murray was so broken-hearted about his tragic loss that he sold Embo in 1913 to the Munro Estate. Stepsisters Janet Taylor Munro and Margaret Hart Martin, after whom Munro Martin Park was named in 1956

Embo at 197-199 Abbott St was the home for many years of the Munro Martin half-sisters before being converted to Calvary Hospital in September 1951. The sisters were this city's most generous philanthropists, leaving many tens of thousands of dollars to schools, charitable and welfare groups when they died. Norman Park was renamed Munro Martin Park in 1956 in appreciation of their generosity.

in recognition of their wonderful philanthropy, lived there for many years. The home was converted to Calvary Hospital in 1951, but was demolished in 1980 when the hospital was modernised. Many other shopfronts and buildings in the CBD and inner city suburbs are not likely to be nominated for heritage listing, but still remind long-time Cairns residents of earlier days. Among them are the former ambulance building on the corner of Grafton and Aplin streets, the former Rex Theatre (302 Sheridan St) and Plaza Theatre (108 Mulgrave Rd) which still stand as they were when many Cairns retirees attended their matinees as children 60 years ago.

It is great that so many buildings remain in Cairns to remind us of the past. But occasionally I yearn for more, so I drive to that part of Cairns where I spent my early childhood in Hartley and Bunda streets. Today the area consists of mainly commercial and light industrial businesses, but my visit brings those years of the 1930s alive once more.

There is little evidence now of what a densely populated residential area this was when its feature was many of those old low-set worker's dwellings, as they were known. Names of families who lived there then flow easily from my memory: Dillon, White, Johns, Graham, Bradford, Burke, Joseph, Clarke, Fox, Franks, Sheppard, Kelly, Gardiner, Vogler, Taylor, Young, Wallace and Brabon. We lived for a year or so at 52 Hartley St, next door to Robinson's store where we bought lollies as kids in the late 1930s.

We played cricket out the front with dozens of other neighbourhood kids, both girls and boys, taking part. Diagonally across to the corner of Hartley and Bunda streets, A.J. Drapers had their furniture factory. Many men from the neighbourhood worked there before the building burnt down in the early 1950s. It was not rebuilt.

A big white house with green trim at 123 Bunda St was off limits to us. Mr W.W. Friend, manager of the adjoining gasworks and his family lived there. His son Henry attended St Josephs School in Draper St. Kids going to Catholic schools were our sworn enemies, but Henry was a mate. He later became deputy mayor of Cairns. On my stroll further

This is the neighbourhood of Cairns where Alan Hudson spent his early childhood with Dutton St in the foreground where Northern Builders Supplies had its premises and *The Cairns Post* its newsprint store to the right, circa 1940s.

down the street, I recalled the day when I had my first drink in a pub. My grandfather Frederick Douglas Hudson had visited us one weekday morning and asked me to walk him up to the Spence St corner to catch his bus.

He took me into the National (now Cape York) Hotel's public bar and I can see myself as an eight-year-old perched on a bar stool enjoying a cold sarsaparilla while he had a beer in one of those glass pots with a handle. A urologist has practised in recent years on the Spence St corner opposite Cape York Hotel, but to me it will always be Lee Moon's Corner. It was where the ever-friendly brothers Vince and Bobby ran their grocery and fruit and vegies store 65 years ago. Around the corner, the line of shopfronts at 151-155 Bunda St look much as they did in the 1940s. Penneys grocery branch store occupied No. 151, and the butcher shop next door was where G.W. (Watty) Wallace, later a Cairns City Council alderman and then Labor member for Cairns, ran the business. No. 155 was Apps's mixed store and next door again the familiar two-storey Apps's flats where the Apps family lived in the front downstairs unit. My brother

Bill and his wife Lena lived in one of the flats at the rear in the early years of their marriage in the 1950s. The flats, a landmark of the area as far as I was concerned, were destroyed by fire in August 2006.

Farther along at 169 Bunda St was where the Hudsons lived for all of my later childhood, when World War II began and ended, through my two years at high school and when I started my first job at the Mulgrave Shire Council. It was also where our family began to break up as my three older siblings, Fred, Betty and Bill, moved out to lead independent lives as young adults. My father, who had left the family home when I was in high school, died in Brisbane in September 1950. My mother died in Cairns Base Hospital in May 1951. Both were a few days past their 50th birthday.

My mother's death brought to a close the family life I had known for 20 years. For the previous year or so I had lived with her and my two younger sisters, Lorna and Marion, in a dingy three-room flat at 2 Lumley St. It was barely 50m from the midwife's house where my life had started on December 24, 1930.

MOMENTS IN TIME

2000 – May 7
State Government purchases 460ha East Trinity property.

2000 – June 27
Sydney's Olympic Torch burns underwater at Agincourt Reef off Port Douglas.

2001 – March 10
NQ Cowboys play first match in Cairns at Cazaly's, losing 32-18 to Penrith.

2002 – March 1
Queen Elizabeth II visits Cairns.

2003 – March 29

Esplanade Lagoon opens.

2004 – August 6
Annual general assembly of the International Association of Congress Centres votes Cairns Convention Centre the winner of their 2004 world's best centre award.

2006 – March 20
Cyclone Larry causes estimated $1.5 billion damage, wreaking most havoc in Innisfail district and southern Tablelands.

2006 – September 4
Crocodile hunter Steve Irwin is killed by

stingray off Port Douglas.

2006 – September 9
Japanese company Daikyo sells last of extensive Cairns property holdings.

2006 – November 19
Tom Hedley, new president of Cairns Jockey Club, shelves moves to relocate racecourse and embarks on plan to upgrade Cannon Park.

2007 – April 2
Thousands of Cairns residents flee city after tsunami warnings broadcast on local radio.

Queen Elizabeth was delighted with the reception in March 2002 from local crowds. She visited Cairns previously in 1954 and 1970.

Reflection

I have, indeed, led a fortunate life in this wonderful city of my birth. I have been blessed with a devoted and lovely wife, a loving family and good friends. My achievements, while relatively modest in the greater scheme of things, have been beyond my boyhood dreams.

We have much to be thankful for to live in such a special place with two natural wonders on our doorstep: the Great Barrier Reef and the huge stands of rainforest reaching from Cardwell north to the Daintree.

This city's future is assured as long as its custodians are never tempted to sacrifice the natural environment for short-term gain. The success of Cairns must never be measured by development and growth, but by the quality of life for people who choose to make their home here.

I have seen Cairns grow from a sleepy tropical outpost to a vibrant, progressive place envied by many. Sure, as an amateur historian, I would love to have seen more of our built history retained, but by and large successive councils have done well to maintain the city so that our special lifestyle has been protected. No gold star, though, for our hillslopes. They should be a pristine backdrop to the city, but housing development has made them the ugliest of eyesores.

I have also been saddened that successive councils have not appreciated the potential of Munro Martin Park. As an historic precinct so centrally located, it should be a place of real beauty, tastefully fenced with ornate gates at its four corners, filled with decorative ponds, flowering shrubs and plants, and with ample paths and seating so that people can spend their leisure hours in a peaceful setting close to the CBD. Maybe one day my dream will be fulfilled.

I have never yearned for personal wealth or to accumulate material assets for myself, but it has been heartening to have witnessed the success of men like George Chapman, John O'Brien and Tom Hedley who have become leaders in Queensland's business world by their enterprise and resourcefulness. Men from modest beginnings like Kev Crathern, John Cleland and Ron Davis, have led this community in another way: as mayors of this city and they have made me proud at how they conducted themselves.

The most satisfying aspect of my life has been seeing hundreds of my fellow Cairnsites lead happy and productive lives. Many have contributed much as volunteers to the well-being of this community, while some have led active public lives supporting causes they were passionate about. And then there have been those who have dedicated themselves to the welfare of people less fortunate. I admire them most of all. They are our unsung heroes.

I am able to look back on my 77 years without regret, only with pride and satisfaction at what my fellow Cairnsites have achieved for themselves and this magnificent city.

Thank you Cairns: it has been a wonderful journey.